Counseling Same-Sex Couples

Counseling Same-Sex Couples

Douglas Carl, Ph.D.

The Atlanta Institute for Family Studies

W. W. NORTON & COMPANY

New York   *London*

First Edition

Library of Congress Cataloging in Publication Data

Carl, Douglas, 1942–
    Counseling same-sex couples / Douglas Carl.
        p.   cm.
    Includes bibliographical references.
    Includes index.
    ISBN 0-393-70107-7
    1. Gay male couples – Counseling of.   2. Gay couples – Counseling
of.   3. Family psychotherapy.   I. Title.
    [DNLM: 1. Family Therapy.   2. Homosexuality.   HQ 76 C278c]
RC558.C32   1990
616.89′156 – dc20
DNLM/DLC
for Library of Congress   90-7288

ISBN 0-393-70107-7

W.W. Norton & Company, Inc., 500 Fifth Avenue, New York, N.Y. 10110
W.W. Norton & Company, Ltd., 37 Great Russell Street, London WC1B 3NU

1 2 3 4 5 6 7 8 9 0

To
Rebecca Lynn Carl
and
William Dan Poole

FOREWORD

Michael Berger

This is an excellent book in a number of different ways; it deserves to attract the attention of several different audiences.

For therapists relatively unfamiliar with the lives and needs of same-sex couples, the book provides a lively multi-level description of same-sex lifestyle issues, supports, and difficulties over the life span.

For new family therapists, the book offers the opportunity to watch an expert family therapist apply basic ideas of family therapy theory – a concern with hierarchy, with triangles, with relationship sequences, with demands for life cycle change – in a detailed way to meet the needs of a specific population. This book will be helpful in giving new therapists clear examples of how to work with families while thinking systemically. For experienced therapists, the book offers the chance to examine the work of a peer, to compare strategies and tactics, and to know that they have allies in their quest to understand and help families.

For many of us as human beings, the book offers the chance to think about couples and ourselves in couples in new ways. We need this because the maps for "marriage" that most of us have, the maps derived from the media (Leave it to Beaver, Father Knows Best, Ozzie and Harriet, The Waltons), from churches, etc., simply do not fit the demography, and therefore the everyday texture of our lives. Too many of us are divorced, remarried, working, homosexual, to fit the map of "couple equals husband and wife and kids, only married once and with wife at home all day."

So we carry with us an outdated map, a poor fit for the

circumstances of our current lives. In the light of the old map, the way we are living, and we ourselves, are wrong. Lacking a map that fits our current circumstances, we are confused and often mistaken.

Dr. Carl's book is useful because he is talking about couples who in the borders of most maps in this culture would be "wrong." Both with these couples and in the book, he works beautifully to suggest that it is more helpful to construct new maps that accept and build upon the different ways in which individuals and couples can thrive than to impose one and only one map on everyone and then abuse ourselves to fit the specifications of that map. Dr. Carl's book offers the hope of some liberation in this regard for both clients and therapists.

A personal note. Dr. Carl wrote this book while he was terminally ill and often in a great deal of pain. The book will stand as a testimony to his work and thinking, to his concern for people, and to the hopefulness that systems theory brought to his work with clients. I am proud to be his colleague.

Michael Berger, Ph.D
Director
The Atlanta Institute for Family Studies

FOREWORD

John Patten

Doug Carl's book *Counseling Same-Sex Couples* is very significant. It fills a huge void in family therapy literature while providing a systemic view of gay men, lesbians, and their relationships.

Much has been written about psychotherapy with gay men and lesbians. But, as Doug Carl points out, "Most people working with gays and lesbians concentrate more on intrapsychic aspects, which, while they may be useful, often are not helpful and efficient in helping people in problems they have encountered." Indeed, these individual, intrapsychic, and developmental models don't seem to help much when applied to problems in relationships. A systemic or family systems model provides a wide enough lens with which to view a couple.

Same-sex couples have to be masters of living in different contexts—both the gay and straight communities, families of origin, families of friends, inside and outside the relationship and so on. AIDS adds another context and complexity.

Gay-sensitive therapist writers have tried valiantly and sincerely to simplify things for us by providing models for understanding same-sex couples. Some of these are well worth reading. Doug Carl does not provide a "model," but shows, through his competent clinical work, how effective the systemic lens can be. We do need models, but they will evolve once the level of the discourse is raised by a book like this.

Like the real world, the publishing world is divided into gay and straight. Gay publishing, though thriving, is "ghettoized." One reason for this book's significance is its publication by a mainstream publishing house, affording it a wider audience.

Ironically, family therapy, which prides itself on being so "systemic," so wide in perspective, has avoided 10% of the population – gay men and lesbians. Is it that a same-sex couple is too far beyond "traditional" for the family therapist? Is it homophobia? Or is it just ignorance of or lack of contact with gay people? Whatever the reasons, Dr. Carl's book will give everyone new confidence and competence.

Thank you, Doug Carl, for being so clear and unpretentious. Your thoughtfulness and great experience shine through.

John Patten, M.D.
Co-director, AIDS Project
Ackerman Institute for Family Therapy

CONTENTS

INTRODUCTION

The AIDS crisis has brought homosexuality into the international spotlight in an unparalleled fashion. No other single event has so raised the world's consciousness about men together (and women together)—their lifestyles, their partners, and their families. Even though the AIDS scourge has left lesbian couples relatively unscathed, the world has become more aware that there are same-sex couples out there. AIDS has also propelled gay men into therapy in unprecedented numbers—to deal with an AIDS diagnosis, to deal with the death of friends, to deal with the illness of partners, to deal with the anxieties of being "worried well," to deal with flabbergasted families, to deal with the survival of the body as well as the spirit.

Yet, most psychotherapists remain remarkably uninformed about the issues pertaining to this diverse population: gay men in a variety of social and economic situations and in various stages of "coming out"; bisexual men, married and unmarried; and lesbians, who remain mostly unaffected physically by AIDS, but find themselves sharing the spotlight and offering their cooperation to the gay male world as never before. Most therapists remain uninformed, too, about the ways gay men and lesbians relate to their families of origin, their networks, and to the world in general.

This is not a book about AIDS, but no one writing a comprehensive book about gay relationships could reasonably fail to tackle the AIDS issue as a major influence. It is a book about the reality of homosexual relationships in a hostile world, and about identifying the real issues, often very different from those of heterosexuals. It is a book geared to making effective therapists even more effective. One important note: *This book is not intended as a book that teaches people how to do couples therapy work – my assumption is that readers already possess some of the skills needed to work with couples generically.*

This book focuses much more heavily on gay male couples than it does on lesbian pairs. If you do not already have an awareness, for example, of the differences between male and female couples, this book will provide useful information in that area. However, my own experience with gay male couples in therapy outweighs my experience with lesbian couples. Still I feel that my experience with lesbian couples in therapy, through observations and interactions in purely social settings, and in discussions with therapists dealing more actively with these women provides a fairly solid background for making useful observations and suggestions relating to clinical practice.

Through the course of 15 years of doing therapy, I have seen well over 75 gay male couples versus about 20 lesbian couples in actual therapy situations. I have seen an additional 100 or so single gay males and 25 or so single lesbians during that time. There have also been group therapy settings with gay men and women, numerous workshops conducted on gay-related issues, and publications produced for professional journals and private distribution.

Most therapists realize that a therapy sample is a skewed sample, so I also bring to this book personal, social observations made over the years with gay men and women and their families in a variety of settings outside the purely professional realm. Their opinions, insights, and observations make up part of this book.

This book maintains a strong systemic orientation. That fact alone distinguishes it from many other books and articles on this subject. A systemic orientation means that this book focuses on context and the circular interrelationships among people in various contexts as determinants of behavior, rather than on individual, linear, intrapsychic factors and explanations. This orientation seems particularly relevant today because the AIDS crisis has brought couple and family relationships under close scrutiny.

After years of clinical practice, supervision, and teaching as part of the Atlanta Institute for Family Studies, my orientation remains staunchly systemic in the modes of Salvador Minuchin (structural family therapy), Jay Haley and Milton Erickson (strategic family therapies), and Murray Bowen (family-of-origin family therapy). My particular approach blends these three systemic stances, and the clinical issues and recommendations spelled out in this book represent this amalgam.

Finally, it is my genuine hope that this book will contribute to the general understanding of relationships in such a way as to promote the acceptance of all productive, functional relationships without regard to the personal sexual orientation of the participants. We all have a lot to learn about relating and surviving, and I have learned a lot about both from gay men and lesbians whom I have known over the years. I thank them!

Counseling Same-Sex Couples

1

DEFINING POPULATIONS AND PRACTICES

For some, the information in this chapter will be familiar. Yet I feel the necessity to supply the reader with some basic information on terms, practices, and lifestyles because I continually encounter experienced, well-trained, well-intentioned therapists who have not had the barest exposure to the concepts and realities of gay/lesbian life.

These misconceptions, however well-meaning, can lead to assumptions that can short-circuit the therapy process or, worse yet, lead a client down a path that will consolidate nonproductive patterns. A lack of definitive knowledge about the populations and practices will sometimes lead a therapist or a client to assume that things work the same way that they do in heterosexual contexts; on the other hand; the therapist may go overboard in making unnecessary allowances so as not to offend a client or not to seem ignorant about the subject. Resources have not generally been available for therapists in this situation.

DEFINITION OF TERMS

We'll start with a pretty basic question. What do you call them? These days, labels are often open to question or confusion, so that is a fair question. Terminology, both formal and

1

informal, is more varied than you might think, so we will go at it by groups.

Gay Males

Men generally prefer the term gay or gay male when outsiders refer to them. Homosexual is acceptable, but carries a more clinical connotation. Terms like faggot, queer, queen, etc., are not acceptable from outsiders, but, not unlike the black population, gay men often refer to each other by otherwise unacceptable labels in playful, endearing, or fraternal ways. Sometimes they are used by fellow gays with hostility. As a therapist, you are safe to stick with gay as a reference term.

Lesbians

For women, the terms are slightly less clear-cut. Most women find lesbian acceptable, but some prefer gay woman or gay female. Others eschew the gay label as a male term. Lesbian women is redundant. Terms such as dyke, diesel dyke, butch, etc., are not acceptable for outsiders, but, once again, they may be used by lesbians. Women in general seem more sensitive to the political implications of terms of address, so remain conscious of general feminist considerations. Lesbians in general are much more politically aware of gender issues than their male counterparts, but this is probably no less true for the male/female population at large. Use lesbian unless otherwise corrected.

Bisexuals

True bisexuals experience sexual attraction to either sex, although not necessarily in equal degrees. The Kinsey Institute researchers identified sexual functioning on a scale of 0 to 6, with 1 representing total heterosexuality, 2 representing basic heterosexuality with a few casual homosexual experiences, 3 representing primary heterosexuality but some homosexual orientation, 4 representing equal homosexual/ heterosexual inclinations and so on to 6.

Bisexuality gets thrown around as a label a good deal by clients who do not know what to do with their strongly homosexual thoughts and feelings and need to hold onto a more acceptable portion of sexuality. As a therapist, you often need to tread carefully around this description, eventually to help the client sort out whether he or she is really dealing with bisexuality or struggling with whether to "come out of the closet." Gay or lesbian identified individuals often express derision for those "AC/DC" individuals who cannot make up their minds. Many gay men are physically capable and even emotionally willing to experience sex with a women given the proper circumstances, but for most this is nothing they crave or aspire to. Obviously, a lesbian's physiology permits her to have heterosexual sex much more easily on a physical level than does a gay man's physiology. However, the common myth that the right heterosexual partner or a "good screw" will tip the balance for homosexuals remains pure myth. (This is a myth that women get saddled with more than men in our male-dominated society. Many men like to think that lesbians can be cured with the application of the experienced penis.)

Transsexuals

Transsexuals often describe themselves as being born into the wrong body; that is, they feel emotionally they are one sex while their bodies are another. For the most part they do not consider themselves homosexual. Many have had the experience of being lumped together with "faggots" or "dykes" by the straight world, and often they resent it. We will not deal with the transsexual population in this book.

Transvestites

Transvestites cross-dress for sexual pleasure. Most are *not* homosexuals but, rather, heterosexuals who derive sexual pleasure from dressing in opposite-sex clothing and carrying out sexual fantasies. They are distinct from drag queens—usually males who cross-dress to act out a feminine inclination or purely for entertainment. Drag queens are homosexual but usually do not report sexual satisfaction from their sometimes elaborate cross-dressing efforts. Some dress to attract heterosexual males and induce them into sexual liaisons. Some drag queens use medical means to enhance the illusion, such as hormone treatments or implants to further develop secondary sex characteristics.

SEXUAL PRACTICES

Obviously, there are some very different sexual practices that may take place between two women and between two men. Also, some practices are the same and may be quite the same as heterosexual practices. Later in the book we will discuss differences based on socialization and roles, but for now it will suffice simply to describe these practices.

Gay Male Practices

Often, heterosexuals ask, "What can they *do* in bed together?" Well, erect penises go into available openings in men as well as in women. Anal intercourse and oral sex remain popular practices, although not necessarily safe practices in this era of AIDS. Mutual masturbation, frottage (rubbing together), manipulation of nipples, kissing, caressing, rimming (tongue in anus), massage, and simultaneous masturbation represent other common practices. Of course, in the gay male world as in the straight world, participants come up with all kinds of sexual variations that may or may not seem acceptable to the population in general. Sadomasochism, scatology, bondage, etc., all have their expression among men as well as among women in their sexual relationships. I have not found a higher degree of these less conventional sexual practices among homosexual men and women than among heterosexuals, but I have seen no research to support this one way or the other.

All of these practices have currency in the heterosexual population in varying degrees (anal intercourse is more prevalent in the *heterosexual* world than most people suspect). Like heterosexual couples, gay couples may play clearly defined sexual roles, although this is not universally true. In some couples, the "top man" is the more active partner who usually (but not all the time) does the inserting, while the "bottom" is the receptor. Some couples vary these roles (called "switch hitting"). Many gay men are quite rigid in terms of their sexual roles, and can experience rejection from a partner if they attempt to step outside a defined role. A top man who decides to take a passive role for the night can risk scorn or future disinterest from a sex partner who wants to see him in the "more masculine" role. Sometimes problems exist for couples when both want to play the same role.

As a therapist, you might reasonably expect less role rigidity in couples where gender differences are not at issue, but this may not be the case.

Other than the standard sexual practices already described, gay males also engage in the less commonplace probably to the same degree as their heterosexual counterparts. Such preferences range from the harmless to the dangerous, from the kinky to the perverse, but I know of no widespread sexual fetishes peculiar to the gay male in particular. Pederasty (boy love), while certainly illegal, is not widespread and basically falls under the same *legal* rubric as heterosexual child abuse or child pornography. Let me emphasize that I have never seen any evidence of organized efforts to recruit boys into a homosexual lifestyle, as often alleged by some fanatical religious groups. There do seem to be some loosely organized pederast networks who share photographs and fantasies.

Group sex and shared sex constitute activities found much more commonly among gay males. From "orgies" in the pre-AIDS days to "safe sex parties" in the present, gay men seem much more available for group sexual experiences and impersonal sexual encounters than do heterosexuals or lesbians. (We will address whys and wherefors in Chapter 3.)

Traditionally, the gay male bath houses provided settings

where almost totally impersonal encounters occurred among individuals either one-on-one or in larger groups. The majority of the bath houses are gone these days, also casualties of AIDS and the need for more responsible sexual practices, but there are still bath houses in major cities throughout the U.S. and Europe. Usually, a person "joins" by paying a set fee at the time of the visit, gets assigned a cubicle or a locker, and then, clad in only a towel, prowls semi-dark corridors for cubicles with open doors and willing participants or other potential sex partners in steam rooms, whirlpools, saunas or showers. Sometimes, large unlit orgy rooms are available for those interested in real anonymity. Generally, sex takes place with little or no discussion between participants, and, once finished, the participants part company.

In the pre-AIDS days, some bars had "back rooms" where men groped each other, engaged in oral sex or occasionally got into full-scale orgies. Again, anonymity marked these encounters for the male participants. Judging by a marked lack of such settings for women, as well as their orientation to sex in general, women appear generally uninterested in these kinds of anonymous sexual encounters.

There exists some research supporting changing sexual practices for gay males. While it is safe to say that many gay males never participated in these more public, impersonal sexual activities, many did. Some still do, but there is growing evidence that drastic changes have taken place: Venereal disease statistics have shown significant declines among gay males, bath houses have closed, back rooms have virtually disappeared, and gay men report changed perceptions and attitudes about acceptable sexual practices.

Unquestionably, the majority of gay sexual liaisons take place behind closed doors in private homes, hotel rooms and the like. But for many reasons gay men have developed other avenues of sexual pursuit, generally much more popular in pre-AIDS times. Most major cities have parks where sexual contacts occur, as well as rest stops on highways, public restrooms, X-rated bookstores and pornographic movie houses. Some of the men who frequent these outlets exhibit sexual compulsiveness. Often, men who are married or single but supposedly "straight" frequent these very anonymous areas for obvious reasons. Many suicides, deep depressions, and panic attacks have followed arrests and discoveries made at these anonymous sites.

The more typical and no less traditional meeting place for gay men has been the gay bar. (Not surprisingly, this spawns a high level of alcohol addiction.) The bar has operated as a kind of cocoon in the gay male culture. Once inside the relative safety of the bar, a man could hug and kiss his friends, act outrageous or just relax without fear of being discovered or persecuted. There, he could meet a man for sex, friendship, or both. Even so, through the years the police would raid bars, haul patrons off to jail on various charges or implement blackmail. In 1969, at a bar in Greenwich Village called the Stonewall, patrons turned on harassing police and caused an all-out riot. This event is celebrated among gays and lesbians alike as a turning point in the right to gather and be themselves. Throughout the 1970s and 1980s, most public officials have softened in their stance toward gay establishments, but harassment still occurs with regularity.

Lesbian Practices

On the whole, women seem more private about their sexual practices. In their homes, they practice cunnilingus, mutual masturbation, manipulation of breasts and nipples, sensual massage, kissing, caressing, etc. Sometimes they use dildoes, as do gay men and straight couples. Outside the home, they shy away from public sexuality: no bath houses or park scenes, meat racks or back rooms. Orgies are uncommon. Impersonal sex is much less the norm; women seem to prefer to know their potential partners first and have sex later. Men may prefer having sex first and possibly getting to know the person afterward.

Women also develop sometimes rigid sex roles, although the stereotypical "butch"/"fem" roles may be more clearly tied to older lesbians or to lower socioeconomic strata. (Better educated, more affluent people in general seem to display less role stereotyping.)

AIDS has left the lesbian population virtually untouched, except in the few cases where a lesbian had sex with an infected male partner. In fact, lesbians have a very low rate of sexually transmitted diseases, unlike their gay male opposites. So lesbian sexual practices have not changed as a direct result of AIDS.

SOCIAL PRACTICES

I have already mentioned the gay bar as a traditional haven and social center; however, this haven is more traditionally male. Women's bars exist, but in much smaller numbers. In Atlanta, for example, of approximately 25 gay bars only three are predominantly female, while the remaining 22 serve men primarily. (In small towns, however, where there may be only one bar, the clientele tends to be much more mixed, with the bar acting more as a community center, especially for the women.) For now, the bars serve a dual function: a kind of social center or club where you can meet your friends, and a place to seek out potential sex partners.

In our culture in general, bars have traditionally been male preserves. Men go drinking together to socialize, while women meet for lunch or at each other's homes. The bar as a "pick-up place" also serves the male inclination toward predatory activity around sex. Historically, women have also had an easier time expressing affection in public, while male expression is scorned. Two women may meet each other and kiss and hug without much public notice. Two men draw stares and comments if they hug and kiss, unless they are foreign or clearly have a familial relationship. Thus, men out of necessity find places to meet that are out of the general public view. Of course, meeting in a bar is also more consistent with the male predilection for sex first, friendship *maybe* later. Bar acquaintance rituals tend to be superficial, perfunctory, and not conducive to really getting to know others.

Lesbians tend to treat sex less casually and seem to have a greater ability to delay gratification. In *The Homosexual Matrix*, Tripp points out that the average male surveyed had had sex with 100 partners, many of them anonymous, while the average female had had sex with 10, most of them known.

Historically, gay and lesbian socializing happened primarily on a private level. A gay "community" did not exist. Rather, you found groups or cliques who socialized in private homes or at the semi-private bars. Newcomers to the scene or young people had no access to any broad social network. The seventies and eighties have witnessed some change, most notably in large urban areas where gays and lesbians tend to congregate. Cities such as Atlanta, Chicago, Miami, New York, San Francisco, Los Angeles, St. Louis and other major urban areas now offer a whole host of organizations and activities: bowling leagues, churches and synagogues, political action organizations, social clubs, AIDS support organizations, etc. Most major metropolitan areas will have at least one gay-oriented publication listing "news," social events, and meetings of various organizations. Still, because of suspicion and anxiety as well as the historical privacy, many gay men in particular do not make use of these resources. And in smaller cities and towns, they just do not exist.

For women, the situation presents different opportunities. Many lesbians became active in the Women's Movement of the '60s and '70s and thereby experienced a degree of acceptance about their orientation that men have not even begun to achieve. Women discussed the issues with each other, debated their sexuality, explored their options. Lesbians became part of a network available to *all* women. For the men, there is no comparable experience. Many "gay centers" or comparable groups now publish directories of organizations and activities available to the gay/lesbian population. These can provide some useful information for the therapist working with isolated clients.

NUMBERS, OCCUPATIONS, STEREOTYPES

In the 1940s, the Kinsey Institute estimated that 10% of the population had a predominantly homosexual orientation (Kinsey, Pomeroy, and Martin, 1948). There is no reason today to believe that is an overestimate. So somewhere over 20 million gay men and women live in the U.S., many of them in secret. Major metropolitan areas account for greater concentrations. In fact, gay populations have often formed the vanguard of restoration efforts in inner-city neighborhoods, since their homes are important to them and most often they do not need to worry about schools. Gay "ghettos" often develop in such areas—providing at least some small measure of insulation from a threatening environment. (Even so, attacks on gays and lackadaisical police protection often seriously mar the serenity of these neighborhoods.)

Many stereotyped attitudes exist about gay men and lesbians, some of them borne out in fact, others not. You will find a high concentration of gay men, for example, in beauty salons and decorator showrooms for a very simple reason: Openly gay males are acceptable to the public in these occupations. Whether or not gay males are intrinsically more creative in these areas remains open to serious question; however, the public expects to see highly visible, more obvious gay men in roles as hairdressers and decorators, so the professions continue to attract more gay men. In these particular professions the gay men interact most often with other gay men or with women, and women tend to harbor much less homophobia than do the straight men in our culture.

But gay men and lesbians of less obvious profiles are also concentrated in other professions that remain less visible and obvious to the public, such as medicine and medical technology, psychotherapy, architecture, real estate, and so on. Of course, this description has an obvious socioeconomic bias. Many lower or lower-middle income gays and lesbians work alongside their straight coworkers largely undetected in factories, auto dealerships, office supply stores, delivery companies, etc. Homosexuality does not know economic boundaries, and it is inaccurate to believe that gay men and lesbians in general are more affluent than any other population. It is true that, since the majority of these individuals and couples do not have children to support, their disposable incomes may be higher than those of couples with children. We cannot know for certain since the Census Bureau does not keep statistics on these groups.

One more word on jobs: Job discrimination is commonplace for gays and lesbians. Most states do not have laws protecting gays and lesbians in the same way that equal opportunity and job protection/discrimination statutes aim at protecting the population in general (more on this in Chapter 3).

Gay and lesbian stereotypes are rampant in both straight and gay worlds. "Flaming queens" more than "diesel dykes" find their way into comedy routines, jokes, and generally derisive conversation. Most of the straight world knows gay men and lesbians purely in these terms. At the opposite extreme, there are gay men playing professional football who could break you in half in a heartbeat. And there are gay women in beauty pageants who can charm their way into the hearts of the most macho males (some drag queens have the same ability). Plus, there are all the lesbians and gays in between these extremes. You simply do not know who they are. You cannot identify most of them because they do not want to be identified, and they mostly create elaborate subterfuge or steadfast distance from colleagues, friends, and families in order to protect themselves from what they perceive as a very unaccepting world.

THE ASPECT OF "COMMUNITY"

People commonly refer to an entity they perceive as the "gay community." It does not exist! In many parts of the country their exists a fairly well developed women's network, which may include support and community for lesbians. For the gay male, especially before the tragic advent of

AIDS, very little network or community has existed. Politicians talk about the "gay vote." In reality, very few communities have been organized to exercise any real political clout. Naive politicians in their ignorance have assumed that gays vote together. Until very recently, they have not. Even more marked has been the inclusion of lesbians and gays in the same description of community. Historically, cooperation has *not* existed between these groups. In fact, hostility has been more commonplace. Gay men have been no less sexist than their straight counterparts, and lesbians have reacted to their attitudes. Both social outlets and political efforts have remained separate on every level except individual friendships.

If there is any silver lining in the AIDS crisis, it is that cooperation has appeared for the first time. For the most part, women have come forward to help out in a national time of need. For the first time in our history, a widespread *community* effort is apparent. Whether or not this will continue post-AIDS, whether the traditional separation between gay men and lesbians will disappear, whether gay men will truly develop some permanent community, remains to be seen.

COMING OUT

Coming out is a much bandied-about term in relation to self-revelation. We will discuss it in a slightly different context in Chapter 3. Basically, coming out means that to some degree or for some purpose, a person with a homosexual orientation reveals himself to one person, many people, and sometimes for the first time to himself. Obviously, different people handle this process in different ways. Some people reveal themselves in very challenging ways, in ways not unlike a "demand bid" in the game of Bridge, requiring a response from other people. Others "come out" to a single person or to a few close friends or family and "stay in the closet" to everyone else in the world. I have asked some clients whether they are "out" and they have replied in the affirmative, but when I have asked, "To whom?" they have replied, "Only to myself!" So clearly the *perception* of where one stands on the sexual orientation issue provides a powerful impetus in one's life. (The opposite situation, where someone is perceived as being gay by others while insisting that he or she is not, can generate noticeable anxiety and undue influence on a person's life.)

There is no way we can deal with the entire range of ways people choose to come out. And then there is the question of whether having a sexual experience with someone of the same sex actually constitutes coming out. My own bias is that it does not, but for some a sexual encounter triggers a certain realization that he or she can accept for whatever it means. (Plenty of people have homosexual experiences they do not accept.) More often it is the physical/emotional realization that may or may not feel acceptable to the individual. Many gay men and lesbians, although living openly with their orientation for years, never reach real acceptance of what life has dealt them.

The actual "event" that marks coming out may be the sexual experience. Ideally it takes place with a sympathetic, sensitive partner, but one can hardly hold onto this ideal any more than one can to the "happily-ever-after" myth. For men the sexual encounter may take place in a locker room, one man's parents' house, a rest stop, a hotel room, etc. Women, once again, tend to choose a more romantic, less predatory setting.

Coming out may *not* involve a sexual experience. People have told me how they came out in their own minds before ever having a homosexual sexual experience. The sex came later or not at all. Incidentally, it does not surprise me that a fairly sizable number of men in the priesthood, women in religious orders, and people in the military have a homosexual orientation. In stands to reason that people who are attracted to others of the same sex might choose vocations where they can be around others of the same sex. Some of them choose to act on this orientation sexually, while others do not.

One thing you can count on with the coming out process: You will find few if any people who have had the opportunity to explore their developing sexuality in the setting of a warm, understanding environment, where homosexuality represented a reasonable choice for all involved.

SUMMARY

This chapter has encompassed largely sociological material that sets the stage in a broad way for working with gay/lesbian relationships. The material is neither complete nor exhaustive, but intended to provide the systems therapist with an overview and orientation to a subculture. In the spirit of good journalistic style, I have attempted to offer some of the "who, what, where, when, and how," primarily leaving the "why" for the next chapter.

2

THE ETIOLOGY OF HOMOSEXUALITY

The question inevitably comes up: What makes someone gay? Clients ask. Families search for reasons. Therapists wonder. As of this moment, no one has the answer (nor do we have the answer for what causes heterosexuality). Still, some valid reasons exist for asking the question and for briefly exploring some of the issues before we talk more specifically about therapy issues.

First reason: Clients will ask you. A number of clients will ask you for your opinion about why they are gay or lesbian. Some ask out of intellectual curiosity. Some ask because they are unhappy with themselves or unhappy with their situations, and they hope that a definitive answer will open up other options for them. Then again, many may have gotten queries from heterosexual friends or from family members who want to understand what makes them different.

Second reason: Family members will ask. If you see family members of homosexual clients, especially parents, they will almost invariably ask you for an explanation. Usually they feel guilty, reasoning that somehow they have done something wrong that "caused" homosexuality. And like all good, well-meaning parents whose child is in therapy, they have come up with hypotheses based on growing up experiences or family strife to explain this "aberration."

Third reason: You or other professionals may consider the

possibilities of changing the sexual orientation of gay clients. Because of your own personal/professional beliefs or requests from family members of clients themselves or your own compassionate response to pain in others, you may feel the need to explore the possibility of changing your client's sexual orientation.

Fourth reason: You want to evaluate significant, recurring family patterns. As a therapists you want to identify family issues that may have a bearing on a client's current behavior, including the relevance of family patterns that consistently relate to presenting problems.

Fifth reason: You or your clients may experience criticism or attack from the religious right wing. Other colleagues or clergy, clients' family members, or even clients may attack your therapy position, since most organized religion considers homosexuality a sin, subject to redemption through spiritual intervention.

Fierce debate has raged among researchers for years about the origins of homosexuality: nature or nurture or a combination of both? The truth is that we do not have definitive information on what determines a person's sexual orientation, be it heterosexual or homosexual. The general public, as well as many therapists, assume that heterosexuality is the norm, and people are just born like that; yet, even Freud (1905) postulated that a person is born without any clearly specific sexual orientation, that early interactions with parents and environment determine the child's future sexual orientation. Freud also remained unshakable in his belief in the inherent bisexuality of not only all humans but also all living creatures (Jones, 1955).

In terms of population figures, heterosexuality is the norm. Somewhere between 90 and 95% of the population is reportedly heterosexual. These estimates only include those people who have claimed one sexual orientation or another, with a few estimates thrown in. We do not have any accurate measures of those individuals who live what looks like a heterosexual lifestyle but whose thoughts, fantasies and desires conform more to a homosexual orientation. And then there are those who share an attraction to opposite-sex as well as same-sex situations.

A good deal of research has investigated the homosexual phenomenon. Most of the research information summarized in this chapter came from a recent literature review of studies relating to male homosexuality supplied to me by James P. Feinberg, Ph.D, to whom I am indebted. Bear in mind that the sum total of all this research indicates that sexual orientation is determined from a multitude of influences, which may prove quite different from person to person.

THE FREUDIAN PERSPECTIVE

Freud (1921) set a definite tone regarding the origins of homosexuality when he introduced the idea that unresolved oedipal conflicts characterized by an overinvolvement with the mother and withdrawal from the father contributed to arrested development and male homosexuality. His thinking was pretty well parallel in the development of homosexuality in women. Men who developed primarily homosexual orientation shunned competition with the father and remained attached to the mother, presumably making the thoughts of sexual contact with other women unpalatable. Normal competition with the father supposedly enables the young male eventually to identify with the adult male image, while frustrating that normal development does not. Similarly, women go through the same pronounced oedipal period in childhood; in normal development, they compete with the mother for the father's attention and then succeed in transferring that love to other males. Instead, with lesbian development, the rivalry with the mother continues, and the girl responds in an exaggerated fashion, as people do when they are disappointed in love, by seeking a female substitute. While the process described by Freud is not always clear, there is no avoiding his conclusion that disrupted development contributes to homosexual orientation (see Jones, 1955, pp. 278–281).

In all fairness, Freud also claimed that external circumstances other than interactions with parents, as well as biological predisposition, affected the development of sexual orientation. Still, the overriding impressions from Freudian thinking are that homosexuality resulted from unsatisfactory relationships between parents or lack of necessary interactional factors during specific critical points in time. (By the way, Freud remarked on how much more conspicuous a part male homosexuality plays in the world than female homosexuality. This chapter reflects that observation.)

The idea that male homosexuality often resulted from strong mothers and absent fathers emerged from this thinking. Homosexuality became defined as a fixation at an immature phase in development. Homosexuality was pathology, and the families that produced homosexuals were pathological.

There are problems inherent in researching this subject from a Freudian perspective: (1) Information is based on individual's self-report of events that often happened many years before and that were colored by childhood perceptions; (2) analytic research often depends on the report of patients, whose views reflect the orientation of their therapists; (3) the information acquired from a subject concerning the nature of a relationship with a parent (a boy's relationship with his father, for example) may be the result of the interaction, rather that the cause of an orientation. In other words, the father's perception that this boy is "different" may influence his reactions to his son, and the son may respond in kind. Nevertheless, researchers have explored various aspects of Freudian theory and the development of a homosexual orientation.

Feinberg cites West (1959) who, based on case histories, concluded that gay males had a higher incidence of unsatisfactory father-son relationships and more intense mother-son configurations. Based on case report, these results are highly biased by the orientation of the therapist and the fact that the subjects were patients.

Bieber et al. (1962) compared fairly equal numbers of gay male and straight male patients. They report that 25% of gay male subjects had mothers who were overinvolved, 75% were overly fearful as children, 50% were socially isolated, and 33% played mostly with girls. Bieber's conclusion, in Feinberg's (1989) words:

> Based upon these results, Bieber et al. (1962) concluded that homosexual sons are enmeshed in parental conflict . . . determined by their parents' unresolved earlier conflicts and transferences. They theorized that these mothers unconsciously identified their homosexual sons with fathers and brothers, whereby homosexual sons became the objects of their incestuous feelings from their own childhoods. Fathers also transferred their own rivalrous feelings toward their own fathers and brothers onto their homosexual sons. The result of the aforementioned triangular conflict is sexual overstimulation, intense, and anxiety in sons regarding their heterosexual feelings, all of which eventually contribute to a homosexual orientation.

Studies like that conducted by Bieber and his colleagues are suspect because the sexual orientation was already known by the researchers. Other studies used samples of one family and generalized from that data. In fact, Evans (1971) reanalyzed some of Bieber et al.'s earlier data and found that some of the homosexual patients had relationships with their mothers and fathers that were similar to those of heterosexual patients.

Other researchers found no support for the idea that nonnormative parent sex-role qualities contributed to male homosexuality. Zuger (1974) found no support for the idea that abnormal parent-child or parent-parent relationships played any part in the development of a homosexual orientation. Despite mixed, contradictory research results, the psychoanalytic community continues to emphasize father absence and maternal overinvolvement in the etiology of homosexuality in men.

Quoting Feinberg again:

> There have been few comprehensive empirical studies on homosexuals which have tested psycho-analytic hypotheses. . . . Much of the existing body of psychoanalytic theory on the etiology of homosexuality has been based upon methodologically deficient studies. A causal relationship between disturbed or good parental relationship for that matter and the development of sexual orientation has not been established. Nor has a particular homosexual (or heterosexual) character type been identified. . . . The lack of classical patterns found in all homosexual males, both in treatment and never in treatment, would seem to suggest the possibilities that clinical homosexual males are inadvertently educated by their therapists and tend to recall their family backgrounds in ways that are consistent with their therapists theoretical perspective . . . and perhaps that numerous routes to sexual orientation may exist.

SOCIAL LEARNING THEORY

According to Feinberg,

> Homosexuality from this perspective is not conceptualized as a pervasive psychiatric disorder but, rather, as a specific set of behaviors which have been learned through social reinforcement, observation of persons and events without direct reinforcement, and/or by the accidental pairing of events during certain critical periods.

If homosexuality can be learned, then it stands to reason that it can be unlearned. Several studies have focused on this issue with mixed results. Adams and Sturgis (1977) suggest that moderately positive results can be achieved using behavioral approaches, but some question exists as to whether their subjects were bisexual to begin with. Other studies suggest that a homosexual orientation is well established from the time of adolescence and proves unresponsive to modification.

As with psychoanalytic investigations, a good many social learning studies use retrospective data. In addition, some social learning theorists have focused their studies on gender-role development, with the implication that boys who identify most strongly with opposite-sex gender roles stand more of a chance of developing homosexual orientations. The problem with this assumption is that once again the data are retrospective, and subjects may report certain attachments that have been influenced by subsequent experiences with society and with the lifestyle stereotypes. Furthermore, Bell, Weinberg, and Hammersmith (1981) report that homosexual males in therapy present a different picture from their nonclinical counterparts. Clinical homosexual males report fathers as more hostile and cold than nonclinical males. Once again, the context influences perceptions with retrospective data.

Although some studies reported by Feinberg seem to demonstrate that certain familial patterns produce male offspring with strong opposite-sex gender identity, they can only suggest that this may be a pattern that contributes to a homosexual orientation. (And, once again, they deal with retrospective reports.) They fail to deal with the fact that the sexual orientation of the child may have already been determined at the time the interactions were studied. They also assume that an opposite-sex gender identification means that a person is predisposed to homosexual activity and that same-sex gender identity precludes the possibility of a homosexual orientation. In neither case is etiology truly addressed. Feinberg reports that while many studies suggest that gender nonconformity is "a strong predictor for subsequent homosexual orientation . . . not all gender nonconforming boys become bisexual or homosexual nor do all male homosexual adults retrospectively report childhoods characterized by gender nonconformity."

Longitudinal studies seem to suffer from lack of standard criteria concerning case selection, age of subjects, and the definition of cross-gender behavior empirically defined. An example of longitudinal findings comes from a study by Green (1976, 1979, 1985), who followed two groups of non-gender-conforming boys. As adults, many more of them became bisexual or homosexual. Other studies support these findings; however, the results are far from universal.

The debate concerning nature or nurture also exists among social learning theorists. Some researchers feel that the early emergence of gender nonconformity and the lack of clear-cut behavioral/environmental findings indicate a congenital origin. Other researchers believe that sexual orientation is at least partly culturally determined. Other studies, such as those by Zuger (1974) and Coates and Person (1985) suggest that a homosexual orientation may be predetermined at birth, with cultural factors activating certain differences from the general population. Obviously, none of these studies addresses the crucial central issue: What determines sexual orientation?

Let me quote Feinberg's conclusions:

> In conclusion, homosexuality appears to develop quite early and appears to be as deeply ingrained as heterosexuality. Although social learning hypotheses seem to have some empirical support, evidence is lacking which directly links childhood learning to subsequent adult sexual orientation. Furthermore, no specific family dynamics have been singled out in the etiology of gender nonconformity. A relationship between gender nonconformity and homosexuality appears to exist for many but not all predominant and exclusive homosexuals. . . . Although the contribution of the child to the quality of the parental relationship, specifically the child's innate characteristics, may affect parental reactions and attitudes toward him (versus parental behavior being the cause of offspring sexual orientation) the

similarities and differences between pre-homosexual and pre-heterosexual boys suggest many different origins of homosexuality and heterosexuality.

BIOLOGICAL FACTORS

Investigation of biological factors and their influences on the development of homosexuality tend to fall into three major categories: (1) biochemical differences as demonstrated by adult subjects; (2) prenatal influences of hormones and nutrition; (3) twin studies.

Several researchers have demonstrated differences between heterosexual and homosexual men on measures of current biochemistry. Kolodny et al. (1971) found lower plasma testosterone and lower sperm counts, with the lowest sperm count among exclusively homosexual men. Testosterone levels for homosexual men who had never had heterosexual experience were lowest of all. Dorner et al. (1975) found a positive estrogen feedback level in a majority of their homosexual subjects, similar, but not identical, to the feedback effect seen in women. But even these differences have not been consistently demonstrated.

Speculation about prenatal influences include the effects of an autoimmune response of the mother to the cells of fetuses (MacCulloch and Waddington, 1981), the endocrinal effects of prenatal stress syndrome (Ellis and Ames, 1987), alcohol and drug use, toxic reactions, and acute illness (Friedman, 1988).

In one study, Ellis et al. (1988) report that mothers of homosexual men had two-and-one-half times higher stress severity scores 9 to 12 months prior to conception, with no relationship between the stress levels and the development of lesbian offspring. Once again, these data are highly retrospective.

Twin studies have classically been used to sort out differences of heredity versus environment. Identical twins raised apart who share common characteristics may prove a case for heredity. Yet, there are some questions concerning differences in hormonal or nutritional effects in utero, even with identical twins.

Limits in our understanding of genetics also inhibit research in this area. Some of the major twin studies rely on literature reviews of past studies, where research methodology was inconsistent.

An often-cited study by Kallman (1952) reports that 100% of identical twins raised apart had the same sexual orientation, while only 42% of fraternal twins shared varying degrees of homosexuality. In contrast, Rainer et al. (1960) and Mesnikoff et al. (1963) suggest that parental attitudes and interactions appeared to determine homosexual orientation in male identical and fraternal twins raised together. Overall twin studies have been inconclusive.

Quoting Feinberg, once again, " . . . no conclusive evidence has been found which links sex hormones in humans to sexual orientation. Nor have postnatal hormonal differences been consistently demonstrated which discriminate heterosexuals from homosexuals. No relationship has been found either between testosterone level and masculinity, femininity or any other psychological variable."

OVERALL CONCLUSIONS

So what can you tell various people who ask, "What makes my son or daughter gay?" The honest answer remains, "I really don't know." The best research we have gives us no definitive answers about the causes of homosexuality. In some ways this can prove comforting. We honestly do not need to prevaricate when it comes to answering the questions of parents, for example. Of course, they may persist in feeling that it is something they did during childhood that caused the homosexuality. (Incidentally, despite all the best information conveyed to parents, it is likely that they will hang onto the idea that their parenting failed in some way, especially the mothers, so share the information you have and don't try to "sell" them until they are ready.) We can say with reasonable assurance that there is no evidence of a single thread that leads to the formation of a homosexual orientation. We can also surmise that someday we may have more answers about the combination of factors that contribute to sexual orientation.

The other advantage of our ignorance is that we really cannot justify spending long hours in therapy probing reasons why someone is gay. Our lack of definitive knowledge in this one area paradoxically supports our need to push ahead and to help couples solve their problems in the here and now. Family-of-origin issues can prove very powerful in the therapy process, but a focus on "what they did to make me go wrong" will go unrewarded.

Some gay clients will want to use the fact of their homosexuality to avoid taking responsibility for their lives. Their sexual orientation becomes an excuse for not pushing ahead or facing issues that perplex them outside of their sexual orientation. We can say to those clients in candor that we are basically powerless to change the facts of life.

3

PRECOUPLING CONSIDERATIONS

By now you should have begun to develop a flavor of some of the sociological and family issues confronting the gay/lesbian population. We have looked some at social and sexual practices that are an everyday part of many lives. We have also sorted through some of the etiological issues in terms of family patterns and biology. These discussion have presented material crucial to an understanding of the *contexts* that gay men and lesbians bring into therapy. But there remain other issues germane to individual development and perceptual/emotional experiences, which constitute crucial elements embedded in the contexts of these clients, their issues as individuals, and their interactions as couples and families.

In this chapter we will follow the thread of issues of individual development, examine the perceptual realities confronting these individuals, and begin to integrate all of this into a systemic scheme for approaching same-sex couples in therapy. We will begin with a look at gender issues, representing the attitudes of a world that we are born into. We will then look at the cutoffs that develop when differences begin to be perceived and issues of adolescent practice.

SOCIALIZATION/GENDER ISSUES

Several years ago, a valued, enlightened, and politically aware female colleague of mine shared an experience that

26

has stuck with me. On this occasion her 16-year-old son was away with a group of high school students on a conducted tour of Europe. My colleague had just gotten off the telephone, transatlantic, with her son. It seems that it had taken some time for the person on the other end of the telephone initially to locate her son, since a party was in full swing on that floor of the hotel. In the background, his mother could hear girls laughing, the clink of glasses and everyone having a good time by the sound of things. "They'll probably get him laid by the end of the summer," she joked good-naturedly, as she got off the telephone. Now, this colleague also has a daughter two years older than her son, and I knew that if it had been her daughter in that situation, she would not have made a joke about her losing her virginity. Not that my colleague is or was particularly prudish, but even to this day sexual values remain different for girls and boys growing up in our culture.

Even though values and sensitivities have shifted somewhat in the last several decades (and may now be shifting back to more traditional directions in this AIDS era), we still maintain different sexual values for the two sexes. Boys get taught to be predators—fathers still secretly or openly swell with pride at the thought of their sons' conquests. Girls are still encouraged to "save themselves" for marriage, even though most parents know that these days few virgins make it to the altar. These values are inculcated in most of us, and since the vast majority of people couple with those of the opposite sex, these values get played out as differences between the sexes.

Of course, these differences in values are not only sexual. In general, one traditional role for females is emotionally to keep the family together, to be "in charge" of dealing with emotions, while men have the task of being tough, dependable providers. These stereotypical but nonetheless potent role ideas have powerful implications for sexual relationships in heterosexual coupling, which often get in the way of potential sexual satisfaction. But for those who couple with others of the same sex, we add a whole different set of variables. Now, instead of a predator coupling with someone who works to keep the home together emotionally (I generalize), we have two predators trying to maintain a relationship. Now, instead of someone taught to be sexually aggressive coupling with a mate taught to be sexually more passive, we have two sexually passive women in the same relationship, who may feel, for example, that there is intrinsically something wrong with sexual aggression or even with sexual instigation.

And thus far we have only discussed one aspect of socialization differences: the overtly sexual ones. What about other divisions of roles in relationships? Pepper Schwartz, the noted sociologist, has remarked that she knows of very few married or cohabiting heterosexual couples who have devised truly equal work-sharing around household tasks and child-raising. Women still usually take the bulk of responsibility for issues of household economy and childrearing, while men still take most of the emotional responsibility for providing family income. (In fact, most couples treat the woman's income as a supplement to the basic family income provided by the man, using the woman's income for special functions such as vacations, investments, luxury items.)

And what about the issues of emotional turf with couples? In general, women in our culture are charged with maintaining the emotional aspects of family life. Men tend to remain more distant. Many women push for more emotional closeness from their husbands or simply accept that they will not get what they need from them. Most men, unlike their female partners, maintain friendships that emotionally have a superficial flavor to them. My former female partner in practice, Carrell Dammann, claims that the issue most men have the most difficulty processing is fear; yet, that is the issue most of them bring into therapy in many unspoken ways. They have no "permission" to share feelings of fear.

This is not to imply that relationships cannot survive if two people both want real emotional closeness or both want distance or they want a real egalitarian stance in terms of household or childrearing responsibilities. It is just that our therapy with heterosexual couples has predisposed us to look at problems from a particular vantage point that may be invalid when working with same-sex couples.

We also need to remember that it is against this backdrop that most children are raised—children who will grow up with a heterosexual orientation, male children and female children receiving clear-cut messages about social expectations. They hear that girls may nurture, express sensitivity, demonstrate artistic talents, remain physically inactive if they choose. Boys displaying these traits get labeled sissy. Girls who display physically competitive traits, who love sports, who eschew the home arts earn the label of tomboy, and tongues may cluck. Underlying these labels lies a rich vein of homophobia: the fear of homosexuality. Even at an early age, parents fear this "deviance" on some level.

From my perspective, homophobia is a fear perpetuated by a male-dominated society. A great many men are locked into rigid role models about masculinity and feminity, and men, much more than women, repudiate anything to do with "sissies." Anything not appropriately "masculine" becomes feminine. Take the house husband, who stays home with children while his wife works. Most men snicker at this situation. There must be something "wrong" with him, and his masculinity is brought into question.

Another very diverse example comes from pornography. Pornography is male-arbitrated. To begin with, most pornography is created to deal with male interests and tastes (the predator again). No evidence exists that men intrinsically respond to pornography more than do women. It is a variable introduced by socialization and what is "proper." (Another colleague of mine expressed shock when her college-age daughter brought home a magazine full of naked men, but she confessed to me, with a good deal of timidity, that she looked at them too!) Then, the content of pornography is dictated by men and their prejudices. For example, pornographic heterosexual materials often feature two women in sexual activity, soon to be joined by a man, who presumably will show them how it is really done. No one has ever brought to my attention material where two heterosexual men provide the prelude to sex with a woman.

For most men, physical contact that contains any hint of sexuality toward another man remains abhorrent in a real or expressed sense. Yet, women have shown acceptance for their sisters who prefer homosexual contact or *who choose it*. Please note that this is probably the only place in this book where I will talk seriously about conscious choice in sexual orientation. There exist a small number of women who have chosen to become what I call political lesbians. They make this choice because they choose not to deal with social/sexual attitudes of men in their intimate lives. *I have never heard of a man even considering such a choice!*

We need to move away from gender issues for the moment, with the clear understanding that this exploration represents a very superficial discussion of gender. Incidentally, family systems theory has generally not incorporated gender issues as part of its approach. Writers such as Virginia Goldner and Carol Gilligan have now begun to remedy that situation. Obviously, we cannot ignore gender issues in dealing with same-sex couples, and we should not ignore them in dealing with *any* sex clients. Gender issues will come up again when we discuss specific strategies for working with couples in therapy.

So we need to accept that boys and girls get born into a world with these standards and attitudes and that they will feel the effects of these judgments on the shape of their developing selves. Breaking out of these predetermined molds is difficult enough if you share the dominant heterosexual orientation. Gays and lesbians shoulder an additional burden, often without their actually realizing it.

EMOTIONAL CUTOFFS

Most, not all, boys and girls growing up gay know during preadolescence, if not sooner, that they feel attraction to the same sex that goes beyond the attachments of their developing heterosexual playmates. I do not wish to make this sound clearly conceptualized. Children and even adults report this as a vague or less-than-clearly-defined feeling most of the time. (I remember a 30-year-old psychology graduate student telling me that, even though he knew that he was attracted to men at about age 11, he had never really done anything about it because he was not aware of what there was to do.) They also learn at an early age that this difference is not valued by those around them. The mother of a client told me that she took her son to see a psychiatrist when he was four because at nursery school he preferred the company of the girls or he wanted to spend time with the adult staff in the kitchen.

One of Murray Bowen's important tenets has to do with emotional cutoffs. When a person pulls back emotionally from his or her family of origin to the point where real emotional interchange is cut off, this creates a situation that shapes the person's relationships outside of the family of origin. The energy required to maintain an emotional cutoff has effects on other aspects of the individual's life. It can, in fact, help dictate the emotional style the person creates for himself or herself. Emotional cutoffs become a major issue in dealing with gay men and lesbians in therapy.

Emotional cutoffs seem to manifest themselves most clearly for the developing gay male and lesbian around the time that sexual urges begin to dominate pubescent life. A number of males have reported in therapy that they engaged in what most see as normal sex play with their male friends. For a short time, they found little unwillingness on the part of other males, but then eventually other boys began to tell them that "they didn't do that anymore." With that overt message came a more covert one: "If you do it, then you're a queer." Women report very little sex play with other girls, once again pointing to socialization differences.

Gay boys now find that they are stuck with a "secret," one that can be difficult to hide. Many of them avoid gym class, locker rooms, or public showers with other boys for fear they will be discovered. They may adopt swaggering heterosexual, adolescent language to hide their real feelings. Some are not so lucky. For the boys who look and act effeminate or for the girls who look and act masculine, there usually is a spate of queer jokes, catcalls, beatings, and pranks. They become ostracized, with no clear peer group to fall back on for support. For all of the adolescents with this secret, there develops a growing gulf between them and family members. The split is part normal adolescence with its turn inward and to peers and part fear of being labeled "different."

Sexual contact with siblings, when it occurs, may simply exacerbate the difficulty. The standard incest taboos creep in, and often embarrassment develops between brothers, sisters, cousins, etc. Once again, this appears to be much more a male issue than a female one.

So most gay and lesbian boys and girls find themselves keeping their own counsel. The lucky ones may find a compatriot. Most parents and school guidance counselors feel inadequate in dealing with this problem. Even if they do show compassion, resources are unknown to them or unavailable in most communities. They usually just imply that the person needs to keep quiet about it or learn to live with it. In most situations, though, the young person never lets anyone know. This may account for more teen suicides than the public generally suspects.

This emerging pattern of emotional cutoff often dominates the life of an adult homosexual, reinforced by the need to remain secretive at work or in the community.

ADOLESCENT PRACTICE ISSUES

Adolescents in our culture go through a nearly universal process of identifying with a group, socializing with that group, and gradually pairing off with opposite-sex partners. Just about all of us go through this process, gay or straight. And, gay or straight, we get our practice in a heterosexual context. For this is truly a "practice period," where, through dating experiences and discussions with peers, we integrate the social skills preached by the adults with the norms emanating from the peer group. Gays and lesbians practice, but primarily they practice heterosexually, even if the interest is not there. (For an entertaining description of someone who practiced openly with his same-sex partner in high school, read Aaron Fricke's *Reflections of a Rock Lobster*.)

For the gay or lesbian adolescent, there is no going steady, sharing adolescent intimacies, or indulging in socially acceptable adolescent sexuality. All the success, disappointment, and practice available to most boys and girls remains inaccessible to the young homosexual, who takes refuge in fantasy or, mostly in the case of boys, in clandestine sexual encounters.

A great many gay men and lesbians search for the same salvation as their heterosexual peers: the fantasy of a prince or princess charming who will provide a life of "happily-ever-after" (a fantasy that seems to me to be as damaging and removed from reality as anything taught in childhood could possibly be). In this quest, it seems to many that gays and lesbians fall in love and out of love with painful regularity. In truth, this happens. But what we often see when someone comes out at 18 or at 50 is a reenactment of the missing adolescent practice period—only we see the practice taking place with adults possessing physically mature bodies, financial resources, and the belief that they know what they are doing. Often, this belief is unfounded. The result is not much different from the adolescent who has a different "serious" boy friend every other month, until she settles down with someone and goes steady. Thirty-year-old men in the process of coming out do not go steady; they move in and set up households, only to see them often fizzle in short order. And, as Mendola (1980) points out, the support framework for practice relationships does not exist in the adult world.

This phenomenon has unfortunate consequences: It promotes cynicism and often despair; it helps perpetuate the idea that gay relationships do not last: it reinforces emotional cutoffs; it activates a negative synergism with an already superficial and transient social network. While we cannot trace gay/lesbian coupling problems solely to the lack of adolescent practice – that would be far too linear – this issue contributes importantly to the understanding of the gay coupling context.

RELIGION

Gay men and lesbians grow up with the same religious training as anyone else, with one important exception. Nowhere does any major religious denomination and the majority of its members condone homosexuality. Many religious bodies condemn it as a sin and an abomination. The gay or lesbian child growing up can get trapped between the religious doctrine of his or her family and the feelings he or she experiences. Mostly this gets interpreted in the form of guilt. In fact, the more fundamentalist Christian churches believe literally in the New Testament dictum that thinking about something that is sinful carries the same weight as doing something sinful. Since many gays and lesbians are reduced to fantasy as their way of controlling what they see as unacceptable behavior, they believe that they are sinning even in their private thoughts. Incidentally, Orthodox Judaism offers no more acceptance of homosexuality than fundamentalist Christianity.

Ironically, many homosexuals are attracted to the religious life not only to control their impulses but, on another level, also to seek an environment where same-sex groups live in close proximity. This is especially true in the Catholic Church, where some sociologists estimate that more than 50 % of some priestly orders are homosexual.

The importance of religion as a factor in therapy varies, of course, family by family and also by region. Religion dominates daily life to a greater degree in the South, where I have drawn a good bit of my experience, than elsewhere in the nation. Still, the Catholic Church represents a relatively small fraction in this part of the country, so the more heavily Catholic North may present more guilt issues around Catholic dogma.

In the last decade or so, gay-oriented churches, synagogues and the like have made their appearance, and they offer an important resource both for the therapist and for the gay man or lesbian, but none of these groups is officially, routinely sanctioned by establishment churches.

MARRIAGE MODELS AND ROLE MODELS

We model our relationships in the heterosexual world after a variety of sources, most notably our parents' relationship or marriages of other family members. In addition, we have role models from the movies, literature, friends, neighbors, etc. We have already pointed out in the example of the graduate student who was unaware of how to pursue his impulses that role models scarcely abound for gays and lesbians. In recent years, the movies *Making Love, Parting Glances, My Beautiful Launderette*, and a handful of made-for-TV offerings have finally provided some positive role identification for same-sex coupling. Still, in the general theme of things, this kind of information has largely been invisible, especially in light of the privacy and secrecy associated with same-sex couples who have been successful in their coupling.

Basically, our ideas about marriage come from hundreds of years of religious, moral, and social concerns about preservation of bloodlines. It would simply be unacceptable not to know who fathered whom in the structure of family life. (Once again, men are socialized to take care of their *own* progeny within the context of a responsible family structure.) Such traditions remain deeply embedded in our white, Anglo-Saxon traditions (which seemed to have been suspended in the treatment of slave families during the 18th and 19th centuries).

The point is that most gays and lesbians grow up with very heterosexual ideas about how relationships should function. We have already discussed in Chapter 1 the gender issues that contribute to different coupling styles. Yet, gays and lesbians often try to force their relationships to fit marriage models: one long-term relationship, growing old together, filling prescribed roles. An important fact for all therapists to remember and to convey to same-sex couples is that opportunity may exist from not having to adhere to traditional marriage models, and less conventional thinking may provide a way to make the relationship work. Living in separate households, living in different cities, serially monogamous relationships, nontraditionally defined roles – all of these possibilities fall outside the normal expectations for marriages and all present opportunities for those willing to get past hidebound ways of thinking (homosexual and heterosexual couples alike). All too often the harried partners see only failure in their inability to stay "married," which adds to the prevailing myths about the viability of these relationships.

Most of us carry around two ideas that we will discuss more fully in the next chapter: (1) that coupling is necessary for happiness; and (2) that long-term relationships are best. Gays and lesbians generally share these conceptions, which may or may not prove helpful in the coupling process.

SOCIAL SUPPORTS AND LIFE EXPERIENCES

By now, you have probably grasped the notion that gays and lesbians do not benefit from traditional social supports. In the next chapter we will elaborate on some of the practical implications of the deficits in supports. You have also probably noted that support has not come readily from peers or "community" within the loosely structured gay/lesbian network. In order to tie together some of these concepts, let us now turn to imaginary scenarios, one for a young gay man and one for a young lesbian.

Michael, 22, grew up in a small town in North Carolina. He graduated from high school and attended almost two years in a junior college before coming to Atlanta a year and a half ago. His parents do not suspect that he is gay. He talks to them on the telephone every few weeks; the conversations are superficial. His sister, recently married, lives in Charlotte. He thinks she knows, but they have never discussed his sexual orientation explicitly. His parents are church-going people who would he feels, be "blown away" if they knew he was gay. He goes home only for major holidays.

In Atlanta, he met John, 23, on the job as a technician in a major hospital. The two of them live with Valerie, also 22, a straight school friend of John's, who likes to hang around with his gay friends. They share a three-bedroom apartment in the midtown section of the city, a popular close-in city neighborhood of old houses mixed with new high rises. Four or five gay bars are within walking distance of home. Michael feels "liberated" because he can openly go out without fear of discovery. At work there are other gay men and women in similar jobs; besides, no one much cares what he does on his own time as long as he does his job. He and John and Valerie go out to the bars two or three times per week. He has a casual network of friends, whom he sees when he goes out.

Michael has had several boy friends since coming to Atlanta. The longest relationship lasted six weeks. Generally, he does not have frequent sex with casual partners, since the AIDS situation has him spooked. Occasionally, he will go home with someone he meets at a bar; unless he's drunk, he tries to stick to "safe sex" guidelines. Sometimes he feels discouraged about finding himself a "husband." He feels confused and uncertain about why two of his "relationships" broke up; the third one ended because his boy friend played around a lot behind his back. But the demise of his last relationship after six weeks has him puzzled.

Joe was older than Michael by three years. He grew up in a far Atlanta suburb, before urban sprawl. Even though his mother lives in the area, she really does not know what his life is like. She dates someone who is "really down on queers," Joe reports. His father is dead.

Michael and Joe met at a bar through some friends. They hit it off right away and slept together two nights later. Sex was "hot," and Michael thought he had really found a "husband." After two weeks of seeing each other almost every night, Michael was ready to leave John and Valerie behind and to move in with Joe. "You'll be back, girl friend," John teased. Joe had been in a yearlong relationship that ended a few months before he met Michael, so Michael could understand why he seemed a bit more cautious.

After a month, Joe really began to distance. They didn't really talk about it, but they began spending less and less time together. Finally, Joe told him that he wanted to see other people and really thought they should "cool it." They could see each other sometimes, he explained. But they didn't, and Michael, hurt but unwilling to show it, avoided Joe when he saw him in the bar, especially when Joe was with someone else.

Michael was beginning to think that maybe his friends were right, maybe gay relationships just don't last.

Joanne, 22, just graduated from a small women's college in the South. She has temporarily taken a studio apartment in the same city where she went to school. She still has social contacts with other women at the school, faculty and undergraduates alike. Her family lives in a medium-sized city some 300 miles away. She has a good relationship with her parents and her younger brother, and she sees them seven or eight times per year. She goes home for the holidays, and her parents visit her when it fits with their plans.

Joanne is not really "out" to anyone, except maybe to herself. She knows several lesbians, and she has listened to them talk and discuss their lifestyles informally at mixed social gatherings. Joanne had two sexual experiences with the same woman at school. This friend has since moved away, and Joanne has just learned that she is engaged to be married. She was somewhat anxious about their sexual contacts, which come after several years of friendship, but the experience was pleasurable enough so that she feels fairly certain that her orientation is lesbian. She has had several sexual experiences with men her age, but she has gotten little satisfaction from them. She especially does not like the male attitude about sex and love versus what she has experienced with a woman.

A faculty member at her alma mater has kind of taken Joanne under her wing. This faculty member is 20 years Joanne's senior and lives with another woman. Joanne feels no sexual interest coming from her older friend, who assumes more of a mentor role.

Joanne feels in limbo. What is her next move? Where does she go from here? She is working to pull lots of issues in her life together: Where does she want to live? What kind of career should she consider? How should she meet people? All the normal considerations of age and place in life face her. And, of course, she faces this other issue that no one has prepared her for.

It is not just the young who suffer from limited experiences and supports. Let's look at two situations where the people involved have had a lot more life experiences than Michael and Joanne.

Alan, 41, was married for 18 years. He and his wife separated last year, after he finally told her about his attraction to men. They have three children, a boy 16, a girl 11, and a boy 8. For the past five years, Mandy, his wife, had complained of a growing distance between them. As the children got older she wanted more and more emotional closeness from Alan, but he moved away instead. During that time he occasionally had sex with men he met at bars or in public places, but these experiences were relatively few because he was concerned about passing disease to Mandy and about any discovery that would jeopardize his career as a successful surgical equipment salesman.

Alan and Mandy tried separation for eight months. Both felt that maybe he would "get this out of his system" if he tried it for a while. Well, actually, Alan knew that these feelings would not go away because they had been there as long as he could remember, but he played along with Mandy's suggestions because he felt that the separation would mean an easier transition for her.

Mandy feels angry and frustrated. If only it were another woman, she would know how to fight it. But this. She has never known anyone homosexual, except maybe for the man who used to cut her hair. She doesn't know exactly what to tell her parents. They are both close to Alan and to the children. Alan has been part of the family now for over 20 years, counting the time they were dating. Alan also does not know what to do about extended family on both sides. His mother is dead, and his father remarried, and they have no idea about his emerging lifestyle. He also has begun to feel the loss of Mandy's family, her parents and brothers, who have provided comfortable, warm support over the years. He feels as if he has betrayed them. He knows that they will withdraw from him when they find out, since they have already pulled back in reaction to the news about the divorce.

Alan also has not figured out what to tell his children. Alan, Jr. is dealing with his own sexual life in what seems like a normal 16-year-old way. What will the news do to him and to the closeness he has with his father? Georgia, his 11-year-old, is an enigma at this point in her life, still part little girl and part adolescent. What will she tell her friends? Sonny, 8, may be too young to really understand, but is he? Kids know a lot these days.

Alan got a furnished studio apartment in a building near town when he moved out. He has an almost 15-mile drive to see his kids on the weekends, but he wanted enough geographical separation to prevent any logistical problems that might arise between old life and new. He still feels very confused about what is going on. He feels uncomfortable sleeping alone, but also uncomfortable with the ever-changing bed partners of the first few months on his own. He feels wounded and still-bleeding from the passionate three-month love affair with Mark, 26, a young man who knew all the twists and turns of gay life because he had lived them since age 16. Alan gave him money, a place to stay, gifts, plenty of attention, and all of his needy, emotional self. Mark took and took and took, and "tricked out" with as many other men as he could get away with. It still isn't over. Alan winces and cries inside every time he sees Mark with someone else at the bar where they met.

Alan also lives in fear that someone at work will see him out. He really isn't afraid of being fired. It's just that after all those years of sneaking around he suffers from rampant paranoia.

Sometimes he feels a cynicism growing inside of him, and he fights it off. He has been out for almost a year now, and he has met a few people, but nothing to replace what he has given up. Somehow he felt that a whole new life would unfold for him just for the asking, but it hasn't happened.

Gloria, 36, married Howard when she was 23, a year out of college. They met through her old college roommate, dated for a year and got married. The marriage was pretty uneventful. They both developed careers—hers as a department store buyer really took off; he practiced law. They had the money to do a lot of what they wanted. They traveled a good bit and lived in a very nice condominium in a large metropolitan area. They had decided from the outset not to have children. They also shared an interest in sports cars and enjoyed going to vintage sports car shows together.

Sexually the marriage did little for her. Not that she hated sex, but she felt indifferent to it. It wasn't just Howard. She had had some sexual experiences in college, and she never could understand what all the fuss was about. Howard liked sex, and she knew he wished that she could respond more passionately. As it was, she did a good job of faking the responses he did see.

Gloria had never had a strong interest in athletics, but when the jogging craze began she found her niche. She became an active runner and even ran in a marathon. She began running with a group of women from work; that was where she met Susan.

They seemed almost to have known each other from a former life when they began to run together. On their long, almost daily early morning jogs, they shared their thoughts and feelings in a way that Gloria used to with several of her college buddies, who had married and moved to other cities. For a year, they knew each other mostly through running and occasional dinners downtown after work. Gloria knew that Susan had sex with men and with women and that she found sex with women a much deeper experience.

One day it just happened. Gloria stopped by Susan's after a running session. It seemed very natural when these two close friends fell passionately into bed. At that moment, Gloria felt her sexuality awaken.

Howard was hurt and furious. How could she have sex with a woman? Was it some failing on his part? His masculine vanity was deeply wounded. They got divorced, and she moved in with Susan not long afterward. Howard was coolly receptive on the telephone, but he still did not understand.

Gloria felt remarkably satisfied both emotionally and sexually living with Susan. It seemed as if this were always meant to be. She fit comfortably with most of Susan's friends. Only her family and their withdrawal from her gave her reason to fret. She felt strangely guilty and conflicted sometimes because she had deserted the values important to her family and because she probably would never have children.

At this point anyone who has any real familiarity with this population could scream, "stereotypes!" To that charge, I plead guilty. The scenarios contain stereotypes and some clichés. My defense is that they will give the reader who is unfamiliar with gays and lesbians some flavor of the isolation, distance, hostility, support, paranoia, etc., which we have covered earlier in the chapter. All readers, please remember that there is a wide variance within this population; however, gays and lesbians share many experiences in common with the people described in these scenarios.

SOCIOECONOMIC FACTORS

Most, but not all, of the information presented so far has been based on white, lower-middle to upper-middle-class populations. Some of the information comes from working with a lower socioeconomic status population, but not a great deal. Some of the information comes from experience with middle- to upper-middle-class blacks, but not a great deal. I have virtually no experience with Hispanics, Orientals or lower socioeconomic black populations. I can only assume that the same hurdles and experiences exist for these subgroups and that the resources available to many gays and lesbians would not prove so accessible to these groups.

Many of the gay men and women in medium to large cities have migrated from small towns in order to find a less hostile environment, more support, and the greater separation between personal and professional lives that a bigger city affords. Although many times small towns tolerate individual deviances quite well, they hardly remain secret! People quickly get labeled and have little chance to create boundaries that might protect their personal lives.

Not long ago, I received a telephone call from a young man living in a very small town in Tennessee. He had been hospitalized in the nearest city briefly for anxiety, confusion, and depression. He had gotten my name from a psychiatrist at the hospital. He lived 150 miles from Atlanta, so coming in for counseling was only a remote possibility for him. He told me that he was 26, gay, and had been involved with a man in his fifties for five or six years. They had kept strictest secrecy, maintaining the ruses that permitted them to operate as straight citizens. He cared a lot for his friend, but he felt he needed to break out of his imprisoning environment. Was there really more opportunity in Atlanta? Could he have gay friends openly there? Would people care if he were gay? He flooded me with questions. But he knew that if he left, he would have to leave behind someone who cared about him and who had been the only support person for his lifestyle. What should he do? A painful dilemma that had no chance of getting worked out long distance!

SUMMARY

This chapter is intended to provide background on people who grow up gay and lesbian. The information we have discussed should set the stage for an understanding of just how the developmental process differs for gay men and women.

The therapist approaching the same-sex couple needs to have a sense of the context or contexts that these clients bring into therapy based on experiences with family of origin, peers, social networks, and everyday realities. This chapter deals with those issues from the standpoint of individuals preparing for the experience of a coupled relationship. The next chapter delves into the realities and practicalities experienced by same-sex couples, realities that often appear quite different from those confronting their heterosexual counterparts.

4

COUPLING ISSUES

Once coupled, gays and lesbians face myriad problems, some not so unlike those experienced by heterosexual couples, some very different. Needless to say, all couples today face the specter of bleak statistics: 48% of all first marriages fail, while 47% of all second marriages end in divorce. We have no accurate figures for same-sex couples. However, in these statistics lies an ingrained prejudice or two that we need to explore before we go any further.

We as a culture seem to assume that coupled is best. True happiness, it is written, lies in wending your way down life's highway together. Real fulfillment, popular myth has it, comes from finding the right mate and designing a life that fits the two of you. I remember as a child that my parents had something of a pitying regard for two groups: those unmarried (particularly women, who certainly would not *choose* to remain single) and those who were married but childless (another condition no person would choose willingly).

Attitudes have changed in the last several decades, but most of us still aspire to finding the one *right* relationship that will help make our lives fulfilling. I find no fault in this aspiration per se, but I prefer to believe that, even though coupling will remain the preferred mode of lifestyle in the foreseeable future, we need to look at it as a popular option among several options open to us. In other words, we do ourselves and our clients a disservice with any implicit assumption that coupling is best. It may prove best for some or for most, but marriage-style coupling does not automatically spell happiness. Many single people can and do find real fulfillment in a variety of lifestyles, but we often fail to credit that fact. In addition, there are those who maintain their coupled relationships in less conventional ways that are rewarding to them; from these individuals we can garner ideas that could expand everyone's options. Some of these ideas will emanate from same-sex couples, who need not always be bound by social conventions, even though sometimes unwittingly they are.

The second myth we often buy into is that longevity is best. As a culture we honor and revere long-surviving marriages. I remember taking a genogram from a client whose grandparents had just celebrated their 60th wedding anniversary. "That's terrific," I exclaimed. "What's so terrific about it?" he replied. "They haven't talked to each other in 20 years!" Less acceptable and less recognized in our culture are serial relationships — a series of shorter-term relationships that may better fill the needs of individuals as they face the demands of fast-moving, ever-changing lifestyles (something that happens quite often in practice without really being recognized). Childless relationships, without the same issues of consistency and stability for the progeny, could sometimes benefit from this serial orientation.

I do not wish to convey the idea that I am anti-marriage or anti-relationship, long-term or otherwise. Far from it! Still, I feel that we do clients a disservice by accepting prevailing ideas of what is best in life and not exploring to the fullest what might work best for *them*. Long-term marriage at the end of the 20th century does not seem to work for large numbers of people. For some, this represents difficulty with commitment or pressures from a rapidly changing world. Perhaps, some feel, the culprit is an erosion of moral/ spiritual values. All these things and more merit exploration. Another option is to evaluate conditions as they appear and to think about relationships in terms of how they might fit changing social conditions.

Gays and lesbians approach relationships with the same preconceptions as prevail in the heterosexual world. Most of them have only marriage models as road maps for how their relationships should function, but these maps, based on a different assessment of the landscape, often lead them and their therapists in the wrong direction.

MARRIAGE: RITUAL, BOUNDARIES, ROLES

Just as it is more difficult to function in the world as a gay individual than it is as a straight individual, it is more difficult to function as a same-sex couple than it is as a heterosexual couple. That is simply reality. One major reason for this has to do with marriage and its deeply rooted implications in our culture.

First, there is marriage ritual. In its most elaborate expression, marriage ritual involves family, friends, church or synagogue, the legal system, and a new status. For same-sex couples there usually is none of this. No planning for the big day by friends, family, coworkers, etc. No parties. No gifts. No introduction of families to each other or to the prospective partner. No ceremony (although a limited number of gay men and women do manage to carry out a ritual ceremony for friends and some family but without any official religious or legal significance). No honeymoon. Often, the joining together just happens gradually, and at some point there is recognition of couple status by the participating individuals through communication about the couple's identity between partners and to others, agreements about sex, and *sometimes* a merging of households. Legally, no state recognizes the union, nor do most official religious institutions (some individual churches will "sanctify" or celebrate the union). There are signs of some small changes in this area. Recently the United Methodist Church voted to accept all members without regard to race, sex, or sexual orientation. And the San Francisco city council passed an ordinance in 1989 that effectively grants spousal equivalency to members of same-sex couples in terms of legal issues of property and employment benefits. Of course, San Francisco is a far cry from the rest of the United States.

More important is what marriage and the surrounding ritual represent. Marriage in our society creates boundaries. It says to family and to the world that there is the beginning of a new nuclear family. Think about traditional ritual: The father of the bride walks her down the aisle, "gives her away" to the bridegroom and then sits down. Families may sooner or later transgress these boundaries, but "right" is on the side of the married partners to conduct their lives as they see fit. Generally, families back off, give them their space, and see them as a separately functioning unit.

For the same-sex couple, bonding often magnifies the issues of emotional cutoffs. It now becomes more difficult to deny one's homosexuality, unless the couple status remains secret. If so, then emotional cutoffs intensify. Often, coupling signals the need to deal with family and friends. *In fact, gays and lesbians may avoid a real commitment because they cannot face that very issue.*

Generally, same-sex couples do not reap the boundary benefits generated by the married couple. Usually, this happens because of lack of recognition of the legitimacy of their relationship. Sometimes it happens just because friends and family simply have not been informed about the significance of the relationship.

Jennifer and Ione had been together nearly three years when they came into therapy. Jennifer struggled with Ione around closeness. After three years, she expected more from her partner. Ione came from an Italian-Catholic family. She had always seen her family as intrusive, and she had worked very hard to fend off what she saw as interfering overtures. In doing so, she had established a pattern she used with her partner, where she defended against closeness that she was afraid would suffocate her (a typical pursuer/distancer paradigm – see Chapter 5).

At my gentle urging, she scheduled a session with her parents. Seeing them together it became clear that the father's motive was to look after his unmarried daughter in his accustomed "old world" way. He knew nothing of his daughter's relationship with Jennifer. Even if he had, there was some question whether he would have respected the boundary created by their relationship. Clearly, he would have treated the relationship differently than he would a "real" marriage. (It is possible in working with such families to "legitimize" the relationship in a way that eventually establishes boundaries between the family of origin and the couple.) This represented a major issue between Jennifer and Ione that definitely called for a broader, systemic approach, which would include additional work with family members, either in person or "on paper" (see Chapter 6).

Pete and Larry were friends, not clients. They had recently celebrated eight years together and generally seemed to have a good, supportive relationship, but not one without friction. A major source of that friction (but certainly not directly cause and effect) involved Pete's relationship with his family of origin. His parents were upper-class Bostonians, with the requisite money and social connections. Even after eight years, they did not recognize Pete and Larry's relationship. It was not clear whether they chose not to or whether they were just naive, because when Pete was in college they found out that Pete and Larry were intimate. That was seven years earlier. They threatened to cut off Pete's tuition and expense money unless the two men stopped sharing an apartment and ceased seeing each other. Pete felt that he had no choice but to present the appearance of compliance. Since that incident, seven years before, there had been no discussion about Larry, Pete's sexual orientation, or his social lifestyle.

For Pete and Larry, the issue still lurked behind the scenes. For that next year in college, they kept the relationship as secret as they could. A year after graduation, they again took up residence together, unbeknownst to Pete's parents. Even now, Larry never answered the telephone in his own apartment for fear that it might be Pete's parents. The parents' shadow continued to influence the relationship from a great distance because Pete's inheritance was at stake.

Larry and his family also played a part in the scenario. They knew about the relationship between the two men and, even though they did not openly support it, at least they showed implicit indifference. Larry could at least mention Pete and their vacations, their friends, and their successes. They all avoided anything that smacked of the conflictual.

Both of Larry's parents were over 70 years old. They had both suffered declining health in recent years, and since they lived five hours by car from their son, they felt free to call on him at any time should they require his presence. During a recent summer Larry had spent six weeks at his parents' home tending to their care and their business affairs when his mother was hospitalized. He spent that six weeks apart from Pete, with only two brief visits between them. Larry's married sister, who lived a bit closer with her husband and child, was never asked by her parents to help.

Both men had boundary issues with families of origin that contributed to tension in their relationship. The tension was not likely to dissipate without some sort of systemic intervention. The prevailing myth was that death would eventually resolve the issues in both families. However, too often the prevailing patterns will continue despite the demise of an older generation.

Tony and Rob would have said that their situation differed a lot from that of Pete and Larry. They had coupled five years ago with the full understanding of both families. Tony's father lived a good distance away and his mother was dead. Rob's family lived within a few miles of the two men, who owned a lovely home in a fashionable city neighborhood. Holidays and family gatherings always found Tony included with Rob's family. Rob had an older brother who lived nearby with his wife. The two brothers and their mates socialized fairly frequently.

Then, suddenly, Rob's father developed cancer. In three months he had died. During the illness and in the time fol-

lowing his death, the family called on Rob for endless er-
rands and commitments and energy, not because this had
been his previous role in the family, but because he was
perceived as being available. On several occasions the message came through loud and clear from his mother, "I would
ask your brother to do it, but he has things to take care of for
Sally."

Whether or not Tony and Rob would have recognized it, in
the final analysis, boundaries held up very much the same in
the two different situations.

We have already touched on roles in our discussion of
gender issues and role models in Chapter 3. In the context of
marriage and couple relationships, we all carry preconceptions of how roles should and do operate. Gay men and lesbians share the same preconceptions, many of which may not
be relevant to their particular contexts: the "supplemental"
nature of the woman's income, the male's primary role as
"breadwinner," the woman's role as primary manager of the
household economy, issues of power and dominance, issues
of emotional support, etc. Although roles in marriage have
changed somewhat in the last several decades, there still
exist fairly clear-cut guidelines and expectations for how
roles sort out in marriage. Sometimes these marital-role expectations cause difficulty for heterosexual couples, such as
when spouses decide to reverse the traditional roles.

One such situation was reported to me several years ago.
A married couple decided over a several-year period and two
children that they would both continue to work, but that she
would focus on advancing her career, while he would just
work a job and take more responsibility for home and kids.
Before too long she had advanced up the corporate ladder
and was making more money than he was. One night a
neighbor dropped by and in the course of conversation in-
quired earnestly, "How can you let your wife make more
money than you do?"

Gay men and lesbians enter relationships without benefit
of clear role expectations because role models remain so in-

visible. There are advantages and disadvantages to this situation. On the plus side, there is much less likelihood that any well-meaning neighbor will inquire about an income differential. On the minus side, there is the push/shove of reinventing the wheel. Through the years I have found that same-sex couples need some help in negotiating these role issues, *but they do not emerge as stated sources of conflict in most relationships*. In fact, the lack of rigid role delineation often leaves room for creativity in these couples.

There may be one important exception. Sociologists Philip Blumstein and Pepper Schwartz have recently come up with some interesting findings in their research on couples. They studied cohabiting and married heterosexual couples and, as controls because they washed out gender differences, gay and lesbian couples. Basically, their research showed that money equals power, that in heterosexual, lesbian, and gay couples, the person making the lesser amount of money deferred to the person making more. The person with the greater income (and status) interrupted more and, among heterosexuals and lesbians, the person with the smaller income generally supported the ideas and opinions of the greater-status mate ("uh-huh, well said, well done"). However, in gay male couples *no one took the supportive role*. Now, because men make more money than women, they generally have more power, too. But even in the small number of heterosexual couples where the woman made more money, the men took something of a supportive role. This seems to say that men will do the supporting for women, but they will not provide this support for other men. This has interesting implications for working with gay male couples, implications that need to be more fully explored.

In Chapter 1 we discussed the sometimes rigid sexual roles observed in gay and lesbian couples. In my experience, these sexual roles do not necessarily carry over into other parts of the relationship. In other words, the man who is sexually passive in a gay relationship does not necessarily assume more traditional feminine duties in other aspects of the relationship. The same seems true for lesbian couples.

For example, issues of household economy, traditionally a female preserve in marriage, may get attended to by either partner (or both), irrespective of roles he or she plays in bed. What you may see is a struggle between two men or two women who *both* want responsibility in this area. I have seldom seen same-sex couples coming into therapy because they could not sort out who would "play" husband and who would "play" wife. The struggle in the sexual arena represents another matter.

THE ISSUE OF CHILDREN

Another qualitative difference exists between same-sex and opposite-sex couples: One will never produce children together, while in the other it is almost always at least a consideration (discounting age). In fact, the opportunity to produce children is a major reason for religious and legal sanction of marriage and a major reason why the culture glorifies long-term relationships. Even the rules surrounding proper conduct in marriage stem from concerns regarding pregnancy and illegitimacy in the bloodline.

Gay males do not couple with the intent of producing children nor will the decision not to have them constitute a common bond. Neither will the presence of children produced in common produce the guilt and conflict present in many divorce situations—making this aspect of separation easier for gay men.

The circumstances for lesbians are changing. Lesbians do have the option of pregnancy, although obviously not for biologically mutual progeny. However, there are at least opportunities to decide together whether to have children. One couple I heard about recently opted to use donor sperm from the brother of one partner to impregnate the other. Biologically, this is as close as one can get to the process in heterosexual unions; even the family bond with the grandchildren is perpetuated.

Adoption has theoretically always been an option for same-sex couples, but in practice this process is extremely difficult for anyone identified as being homosexual. Adoption, in fact, may prove a tortuous process for qualifying heterosexual couples.

Still, the vast majority of gay and lesbian couples do not make conscious or even subconscious decisions to have children, and this fact means that this bonding factor is unavailable to them.

It is not unusual for one or both partners in gay or lesbian relationships to bring children from a marriage into the same-sex relationship. Such an arrangement brings up two major issues, one common to heterosexual recouplings and one unique to same-sex marriages. The universal blended family issues present in all recombinations present a force to be reckoned with for homosexuals and heterosexuals alike, but the issue of how and when to deal with children around your sexual orientation represents a distinctly homosexual problem.

Many books have already been written on the challenges and strategies of dealing with blended family issues. We will deal with some of them briefly in Chapter 7. Much less has been explored concerning coming out to the children and all of the implications involved in that process. We will devote more discussion to these clinical issues in Chapter 7.

As a therapist, I have also experienced a much more subtle issue impacting same-sex couples, one that may affect gay males more than lesbians. I have been impressed with a qualitative difference between gay men who have been married, especially those who have been married with children, and those who have never experienced heterosexual marriages. When you think about it, the implications are obvious: Those who have been married have experienced firsthand all the supports and role expectations that go with marriage in our culture. So it is not surprising that their expectations in gay relationships come tinged with these feelings and attitudes.

Darryl and Don split up after five years together. The breakup was congenial and could be traced to a number of issues. A major, largely unspoken, issue involved Don's incomprehension of the powerful emotional bond that existed between Darryl and his ex-wife and child. In fact, Darryl, who had maintained a very positive relationship with his ex-wife, admitted that when he visited them in their home town, he enjoyed the three of them going out as a family, just like in the old days. "Kind of like having your cake and eating it, too," he exclaimed. Don did not resent this bond intellectually, but emotionally it upset him quite a bit. He felt on the outside of a major force in Darryl's life – and, in truth, he was.

Many major cities have support groups or networks for gays and lesbians who have been married, since so often they feel out of sync with never-married gays. "I feel so much better understood around other gay men with kids," Darryl reported. While lesbians may feel just as strongly about this kind of support or lack of it, this has not represented my experience with them. Somehow it *may* be that, since women tend to be more child-focused as a group, there exists more support and understanding in the lesbian culture in general.

DUAL CAREERS

The vast majority of same-sex couples face the issues of dual careers that many heterosexual marriages face. (This is one area where a heterosexual relationship issue, one that has received a good deal of attention in recent years, *does* generalize to the same-sex couple.) Almost always, both participants in a same-sex relationship work at jobs or careers rather than one person staying home as homemaker. Some of the issues confronting any dual-career couple concern where to locate or relocate, coordination of work and time together, and satisfaction from long-term career goals (see Berger, Foster, and Wallston, 1978).

In many dual-career marriages, the traditional obstacles of male/female position and status in the marriage plus the demands on one spouse to combine childcare, housework, and career provide fodder for conflict and cry out for resolution. Gay male and lesbian unions do not have to face these concerns. Same-sex couples, though, may experience an obstacle concerning the fruits of their labors, since, because of previous experiences and sociological conditions discussed earlier, there is not necessarily the assumption that "what's mine is ours," as one tends to find in a marriage. In fact, the rampant cynicism concerning lack of permanence in these relationships also contributes to difficulties in sharing resources. However, sometimes the reverse is true: A couple works so hard to stay together just to show that it *can* be done and resources are shared so completely that there is little room for individual use of financial resources (perhaps an extreme embrace of traditional marital values).

Jay, who earned $35,000 per year, complained that he could not even buy a shirt that he might see and want because there was no money left over from the joint budget administered by his lover, Steve, who earned considerably less. These two men adhered strongly to a fairly traditional marital household management philosophy, but there was still resentment caused by the disparity in incomes. The "what's mine is ours" dictum did not work for them, even though they tried to operate like a traditional marriage in many ways.

Another major issue common to dual-career couples is the "whither thou goest" dilemma. Traditionally, families move when the husband gets transferred, but with a more professionally egalitarian arrangement couples need to prepare to decide when career demands for *either* spouse may dictate a move. Over the years, I have seen a small number of gay male couples split up over this issue: "It was time for us to go our separate ways anyway," Charles said. "We'd been together four years and things were starting to feel stale. We had more time together than most of my friends have had, after all." This couple split when Charles' lover, Phil, took a job across the country. Charles was not willing to give up his job and his friends to make the move. Their expectations regarding impermanence of gay relationships also contributed to the outcome.

This issue may take a slightly different twist for lesbians, since in traditional marriages women most often give in around this issue. Lesbians may struggle with whether they have the *right* to ask a partner to move, while men may assume they have the right implicitly. As was discussed earlier, men also tend to display more open competitiveness around professional accomplishments than their lesbian counterparts, making their actual process around this issue a more vigorous and even hostile one. Coupled men with unequal incomes and potentials will likely experience competition and friction eventually.

THE FUSION ISSUE

The gender issues discussed in Chapter 3 also get played out in relationship styles that are fundamentally different for gay men and for lesbians. We have hinted at some of this operating in other areas, such as dual careers and support for having children. A more basic difference seems to operate in terms of style.

Krestan and Bepko, in a classic 1980 *Family Process* article, present the case for what they call "lesbian fusion." According to the authors, women's socialization tends to make them more homebound, to erode boundaries between them, and to fuse them dysfunctionally under stress. They describe this as a "two against the world" posture. Men, on the other hand, tend to distance under stress, staying away from home, involving themselves in other activities, including sexual ones.

This major difference really is not too surprising when we consider that women in our culture tend to be the ones who hold families together, keeping the home fires burning and providing the lion's share of the emotional support in families. Men are the ones who typically go out to earn a living and to intermingle with a broader world. These differences manifest themselves markedly in therapy, which we will discuss later in more detail.

INTRA-RELATIONSHIP DIFFERENCES

Several years ago, one of my partners asked me this question: "How come," she said, "most of the heterosexual couples I see come from the same or similar socioeconomic background, and so many of the gay couples I see come from such unlike backgrounds?" I do not know whether her observations would hold up statistically, but my observations have been somewhat the same. Seemingly, more gays and lesbians come from dissimilar cultural, educational, and economic backgrounds. If this is true, we might attribute it to the fact that the pool of available partners is smaller for gays and lesbians and *as a group gay men and lesbians are thrown together only because they share the same "deviant" sexual orientation*. So the son of a sharecropper from Alabama finds himself in a bar with a corporate attorney's son from New York. They find each other attractive, have sex, and may end up as a couple. Since meeting places for gay men in particular have been limited and reasonably isolated, the selection of partners of unlike backgrounds becomes more likely.

Another observation that may not hold up statistically: I have observed more same-sex relationships with fairly great differences in age than I have in heterosexual relationships. The need for role models in the coming-out process, cutoffs from family, the small pool of eligible partners, and various other reasons may account for this phenomenon. For the therapist, it means another consideration in therapy: different experiences and developmental stages.

Interracial considerations may also play more of a part in therapy. In Atlanta, for example, an organization called Black and White Men Together provides support for a fairly sizable number of interracial couples. Interracial coupling should logically be easier with gays and lesbians, since so many are already cut off from families of origin and having children is usually not a major consideration.

LEGAL ISSUES

There are few legal protections for same-sex couples. Their sexual acts are illegal in most states. They may not file joint income tax returns, claim each other as deductions, qualify as dependents on insurance policies, collect a "spouse's" Social Security, or, in some cases, be named as life insurance beneficiaries. We have mentioned the difficulty with adoption. Gays and lesbians may be barred from visitation with their own biological children, and they experience difficulty gaining custody in divorce proceedings.

Monty, 34, had been married for eight years and divorced over three. He has three children, two sons, nine and seven, and a daughter, four. Since the divorce, his middle child, Alex, has presented problems for his mother. She has remarried and lives 150 miles from her ex-husband. Whenever Alex becomes particularly difficult, his mother sends him to his father to live. Sometimes this has happened with advance notice, sometimes more spontaneously. After several months, she misses Alex, feels guilty about abandoning him to his father, and takes steps to get him back. Since she never has surrendered custody, this gets accomplished with little difficulty. Monty has repeatedly asked for custody, but his ex-wife always puts him off. He is afraid to go to court because the issue of his homosexuality may come up and, in his old home town, there is some likelihood that the judge would deny visitation altogether. Obviously this situation is detrimental to Alex. It also puts a burden on Monty's relationship with his partner, since the blended family issues never really get addressed (see Chapter 7).

AIDS has sharpened the focus on legal protections or rights for spouses. Anecdotal information is replete with examples of a surviving spouse losing everything the two of them had worked for to a deceased lover's next of kin. For most couples, where one partner has contracted AIDS, negotiation around wills, power of attorney, use of life support measures, and legal issues around death and burial becomes essential in the relationship.

In general, same-sex couples must work at what married couples take for granted as legal rights. Of course, the absence of legal bonds makes it easier for partners to move on with relative legal ease. It may also contribute to the attitude of not really taking the relationship seriously. Some couples may use legal commitments such as joint ownership of property, wills, and life insurance to formalize their bonds.

SUMMARY

This chapter has presented an overview of many of the issues particularly germane to same-sex couples. In the next chapter, we shift from the sociological to more therapy-specific topics. We begin with a consideration of theoretical issues involved in couple counseling in general and with same-sex couples in particular.

5

SOME THEORETICAL AND PRACTICAL ISSUES IN COUPLES COUNSELING

After years of practice, my orientation remains staunchly systemic. That is to say that I feel that understanding of and solution to human problems occur most readily by assuming a contextual view. More traditional intrapsychic psychology assumes that people do what they do because of what goes on in their heads *individually* – largely irrespective of context. Ideas, behaviors, and structures get fixed in individual heads, and these "personality constructs" determine their behavior. An analogy might be to a tape recording playing upstairs that colors all the perceptions, thoughts, and actions of the individual, with little change from setting to setting.

Systems theory disputes this orientation. Systems theory posits that actions of individuals are determined by the contexts in which they find themselves. Contexts create demands for people to play roles that fit with roles that others play in the same context. Take someone out of a particular context, "therapize" him or her, and return that person to the context, and the individual will immediately begin to conform to that context once again – unless, of course, the person has been properly coached on changing his or her roles. A good example occurs in an alcoholic system, where you have the addicted person, a person who enables the drinking through protecting the drinker, a parentified child who has assumed adult duties in the family, a distractor who keeps the family focus away from the drinking behavior, etc. Pluck the alcoholic from that system and put him into a treatment setting, and he may stop drinking. However, if the rest of the system does not change, he will most probably begin drinking again soon because the system as constituted needs a drinker in order for the other people to continue to play the roles with which they are comfortable. In other words, you cannot understand behavior by studying the *parts* of a system because the parts only make sense in the *context* of the *whole*. The whole, therefore, is greater than the sum of the individual parts.

According to systems theory, people do develop a repertoire of roles, which change from system to system. It is conceivable that the mild-mannered school janitor could be a virtual autocrat in his own home. In the school setting, his position in the *hierarchy* may be quite low, so he assumes a role at school that is consistent with the role expectations for his position. At home, his hierarchical position changes. He has the potential to operate at the top of the hierarchy, which he does with resultant autocratic behavior. Now if you were to study his "personality" at school, you would come up with one profile. And if you studied his "personality" at home, you would come up with another. And if you examined his "personality" as an individual patient in your office, you might come up with a third. Most of us who work systematically have had the experience of having someone referred with a particular psychological evaluation that makes him look quite disturbed, but who looks quite functional when he is seen in the context of his family.

Another characteristic of systems theory is its *circularity*. Most psychological theory is linear: It says A leads to B leads to C. Linear causality does not fit with systems theory, which says that interactions happen in a way that stimulates other interactions, almost as in a circle, where there is no starting point. In addition, these interactions feed back to other interactions in cybernetic feedback loops. So a systems therapist never assumes that some event "caused" a symptom. Rather, it is assumed that every symptom has a function within a system that benefits the balance of the system as well as benefiting the individuals in the system. This is a concept that requires some real thought and understanding because it implies that, no matter how severe a symptom or behavior looks, it only continues if it benefits the system homeostasis and provides something "needed" to the person exhibiting the behavior. So the depressed mother's symptom helps to balance the family system as well as to deliver something that benefits her in some way.

Human systems are open systems, which means that other systems overlap and interact with them. A family system is influenced by school systems, work systems, the legal system, social systems, etc., which may have a very powerful impact on what is happening in the family. So the systems therapist must have knowledge about extended family, workplace, cultural pressures, developmental issues, etc. This is not a theory comfortable with just you and me in an office.

Systems theory has little room for blame. Determining who might be at fault is linear and goes nowhere. Consequently, standard diagnostic nomenclature has no place in systems work, since it labels people negatively and implies that their behavior is fixed and predetermined by prior events. Systems therapists work to develop "positive frames" for behaviors and interactions, looking at their functions in stabilizing a system in a particular way, even when the outcome might be dysfunctional for individuals in the system. The therapist then works to help the system adjust in ways that provide more functional interactions and behaviors.

The concept of *hierarchy* becomes essential in systems work. Dysfunction always follows from violations of acceptable hierarchy, and the therapist works to reestablish hierarchy and *boundaries* between people in the system that permit more positive results for everyone involved. The structural family therapy of Salvador Minuchin (1974) best embodies this approach.

Systems therapists also look for *triangles* as evidence of dysfunction. Murray Bowen states that a two-person system under stress tends to bring in a third party to form a triangle. The triangle then diffuses the tension between the two, but it usually also creates some dysfunctional behavior. Bowen and his adherents work closely with multigenerational family-of-origin issues. They work on the principle that many roles are passed down through the generations. Their family history *genograms* map family patterns over several generations. Working with genograms becomes an important tool in counseling couples, heterosexual and homosexual. The definitive book on genograms is *Genograms in Family Assessment* by Monica McGoldrick and Randy Gerson.

MY ORIENTATION

My own work with families, couples, and individuals integrates the thoughts of three major systems theories: family-of-origin work represented by Murray Bowen, the structural family therapy of Salvador Minuchin, and strategic family therapy based on the work of Milton Erickson and Jay Haley. In addition, my graduate work focused heavily on the more traditional thinking of Erik Erikson, and his stepwise developmental scheme is important in my work as well.

I can best sum up the integration of this work as follows: When working with families and couples, I am first concerned with hierarchy issues. Who is on top? What kind of boundaries exist between subsystems and within subsystems? Do cross-generational coalitions and other forms of triangulation exist? In other words, my initial assessment is strongly structural. I have a map in my mind of what the family or couple "should" look like. And this map is based on the *life cycle position* of the family and the people within the family.

The life cycle issues in a family often result in a complex

interaction of forces determined by individual life cycle issues of the members. For example, the emerging adolescent
concerns of a 13-year-old girl interact with and stimulate the
midlife issues of her 40-year-old mother, which may pull at
the father in the midst of his own midlife career issues,
which affects the reemerging issues of couple identity, etc.
In fact, whenever I feel "stuck" with a couple or with a family, I focus more closely on developmental concerns and almost always find a way to get unstuck. The life cycle issues
help to conjure up this map of how the family "should" look.
In this case, the adolescent has become more disengaged
from the family as peer relationships assume their age-ap-
propriate importance. Boundaries between the adolescent
and her parents become somewhat more rigid. At the same
time, adolescence requires that appropriate boundaries exist
in the *executive subsystem*, so that the parents may function as a team during an often trying transition. Often, but
not always, their functioning as an executive team influences their functioning as a *spousal subsystem* and vice ver-
sa. These transitional issues and the chaos they create often
are what brings people into therapy.

Since the family system does not operate in isolation, I
spend time assessing how *outside influences* in the form of
overlapping systems affect the functioning and flexibility of
the family. School, work, neighborhood, the law, social network, extended family, etc., can work powerfully for the good
or the detriment of the family or couple.

Finally, I consider *subcultural differences*. Maps must be
adjusted according to any subcultural differences that exist
for a family. For example, a Serbian friend of mine had lived
in the U.S. for eight years with his wife and two young children. They had emigrated as a nuclear family unit without
any extended family or friends. They experienced strain as a
family because the husband and wife never spent time as a
couple without the children. The obvious solution – a social
life for them – had deeper implications because in their culture there is no such thing as a babysitter. Children are en-
trusted only to family members for watching. They had no

other family members within 4,000 miles! Other, less obvious differences exist for families based on geographical area of the country, religion, national origin, race, etc.

These four factors—hierarchy, life cycle, outside influences, subcultural differences—make up the backbone of my assessment orientation, but there are other factors of importance, too. When working with couples (and with individuals), family-of-origin work assumes more importance. Couple and individual work takes place over longer periods of time for me than does symptom-focused or child-focused family work. With couples, we need to examine family patterns and roles that can get passed down through the generations. Family styles differ, often dramatically, making mutual perceptions difficult. Loss or trauma, divorce or lack of divorce, family size, history of alcoholism, etc.—all have a strong bearing on the functioning of a couple. Often, couple therapy involves individuals working to change the roles they have always played in their families of origin in order for their functioning as spouses to change.

Sequences of behavior in all of their ingrained glory often provide an essential clue to the dysfunctional couple's difficulties. The therapist's skill in breaking into dysfunctional sequences can determine success or failure in couple work.

You will notice that communication theory does not appear at the top of my therapeutic hierarchy. Communication theory and expression of feelings have their places in couple work, but not nearly to the extent pushed by many therapists and the popular press. Communicating thoughts and feelings can be positive and rewarding in a relationship, but too often communications get caught up in distorted hierarchy or unrelenting, rigidly limiting sequences. We all know people who express feelings *ad nauseum*, even though that expression makes not the slightest change in their lives. There is no question that sometimes people come into therapy with no real understanding of how to talk to each other. Training in active listening and self-expression can help some of these clients, but only when the decks are cleared of interfering baggage. Some people just need to learn how to talk to their spouses, but cases like these are rare these days because of exposure to books and guests on TV talk shows that have encouraged self-expression as one of the keys to a fulfilling life.

One communications approach does stand out, and I use some of its precepts from time to time. I am speaking of neurolinguistic programming, or NLP (Bandler and Grinder, 1975). The NLP folks venture that we all have primary sensory modalities that influence our communications (some of us are visual, some auditory, some kinesthetic, etc.) and that under stress people with different primary modes miss each other's communications. I saw a couple a few years back where one member wanted to *hear* expressions of caring, while the other one had to *see* these expressions in order to be convinced. So when the auditory person failed to take out the trash or pick up his clothes, the visual person could not be convinced of his sincerity no matter how many times he *said* he cared. The same thing happened in the other direction when the visual person never told his partner that he cared—all his efforts to *show him* otherwise went for naught.

COUPLE WORK—A DIFFERENT ANIMAL

This chapter is not intended to survey the important theories that relate to effective couples work, but rather to give you a flavor of the influences that affect my work in particular. To that end, I feel that it is appropriate to comment here that, of all the different therapy modalities and combinations of treatment possibilities, there is less *theory* specifically relevant to couples work than to any other area of psychotherapy. We have coherent theories for dealing with families, individuals, groups, networks, etc., but it appears to me that couples work is a slightly different animal from all the others. And, for me, no particular theory of couple therapy stands out as definitive or predominant in the therapy lexicon. This is my personal view only, and I acknowledge that some writers have tackled this subject far more effec-

tively than others. Nevertheless, no theory has come forward for couples work in the same way as, say, structural
family therapy has emerged for child-focused family work.

I have mentioned that I see couples work as a slightly
different animal from other therapies. Let me explore some
of the differences as I see them.

To begin with, we need to distinguish between relationship-oriented therapy and symptom-oriented couples therapy. Relationship-oriented couples therapy deals with interactional relationship issues between two individuals who have
entered into a significant commitment at some point along
the line. Symptom-focused couples therapy deals with what
is traditionally defined as an individual problem (depression,
anxiety, etc.) within the context of a relationship – in true
systemic fashion. Often, symptom-focused couples therapy
turns into relationship-focused couples therapy, but the focuses differ for the therapist. In terms of this book, we will
deal primarily with relationship-focused couples therapy, except in Chapter 8, where we discuss working with AIDS, a
variant of symptom-focused couples therapy.

Next, we need to look at what I consider a subtle difference between couples therapy and family therapy or individual therapy. Sometimes I find this difference difficult to convey because for me the difference is a subtle one concerning
the *flavor* of the therapy. Let me try to sum it up by saying
that in couples therapy there is almost always the threat
that someone will leave, that one or both people have the
power to get out of the relationship. That threat (or perhaps
option would be a better word) is conveyed overtly or covertly between the two people. In addition, it is an option that
usually can be exercised unilaterally – one person can just
say, "I am leaving." Plus the leaving can take place just because one person does not feel right about the relationship
any longer. "I don't love you anymore, and I want to be in a
relationship where I feel love," is a lament heard often by
those who do couples work. Sometimes, to the other party's
frustration, it can be demonstrated that "on paper" the

relationship has all the elements needed for success, yet the elusive "feeling element" is missing, and its absence is enough to end the relationship. The other partner is left with little recourse except to comply. Of course, *both* parties may decide that the spark is gone and that neither wants to continue.

This "discontinuance option" does not come into play as a major force in most other therapies. Few families coming into therapy with a child-focused problem have the option of getting rid of the child if the problem does not get solved. Even when families choose to send a child away in some fashion, usually they must maintain some form of responsibility for the relationship with the child. Dissolution of a relationship with a serious commitment component can move from deepest intimacy to complete cutoff in a relatively short period of time, whereas the blood connection to offspring usually remains on some emotional level. Neither does the "discontinuance option" come into play in individual therapy. A person coming into individual therapy with what he or she defines as an "individual problem" (an incomplete definition in my opinion) does not have the option of leaving the problem, unless the problem is another person or unless the person uses suicide as an option. When suicide is threatened, though, we have legal and spiritual leverage that usually helps to prevent the exercise of that option.

As a therapist seeing couples, I take another position that may seem foreign to other therapists. I am *not* a marriage counselor. I am a couple therapist. This is a distinction that I make clear to my couple clients. What I mean by this is that I do not take a professional position on whether a couple should stay together or split up. I tell all couples that I can help them to stay together, if that is what they choose, and I can just as effectively help them to come apart constructively if they choose that option. This position has several important ramifications: It enables me to avoid becoming incorporated into a system on one side or the other; it keeps me from putting my energy into a position that may not be endorsed by the couple and that may represent an emotional response on my part rather than a sound professional stance; it expands the options that I can introduce to break into unproductive sequences. Perhaps this last factor is the most important, since it helps me deal in a straightforward fashion with more options and without so much walking on eggs where separation is concerned.

The truth is that most of us want to help keep relationships together unless we see something in them that is really destructive to one or both parties. Yet, effective therapy with a couple also means providing the tools to help people split up effectively, completely, and with as few loose ends as possible. Parting with the potential to remain friends and/or with the feeling that the relationship represents a closed chapter but a productive one is one of many responses that can emanate from a good "uncoupling" process.

For couples with children, an issue for separating is whether they can maintain their positions as managers of the children, even when they cannot or do not choose to maintain their roles as spouses. Many couples are learning in divorce that they can maintain high levels of cooperation around child-management issues.

Another initial consideration in treatment involves what constitutes a couple. One gay client years ago asked me if he could bring in his boy friend of three weeks for couple counseling. Another man and woman showed up for an initial session only to tell me that each was married to someone else and that the two of them were having problems within their affair. A female client asked to bring in a longstanding boy friend in an attempt to pressure him to make a commitment to her.

Make no mistakes about it — seeing people in couples therapy puts pressure on that relationship, both in the form of scrutiny and in the form of emotional expectations surrounding their status. So the gay client who had already demonstrated his need for "adolescent practice" was discouraged from bringing in his new boy friend for two reasons: (1) The relationship per se did not really exist yet; and (2) seeing them as a couple at this stage would put too much pressure on them too fast and encourage them to look at the relationship in ways that might prove unproductive. The two "affairees" were told that they were both locked in triangles that would make couples work unproductive, and that resolution of their particular problems must involve unsuspecting spouses, who certainly would react unfavorably to any "group" therapy. The female client understood that I would see her with her friend, but only with the understanding that she presented her agenda clearly to him.

People come into couples therapy with other agendas. One fairly popular one is to make sure that the spouse will be okay or cared for by the therapist when the other spouse leaves, which he or she has already decided to do. Another agenda involves labeling the partner as "sick" or "disturbed" in order to justify leaving or carrying on an affair. Another involves creating the appearance of having tried everything, so that uncoupling can occur with less guilt or more rationalization. I do not mean to sound judgmental about such agendas; however, the couple therapist needs to be attuned to these and many more and to avoid forming a coalition with one spouse against the other.

The issue of secrets almost always comes up in couples work. As a therapist I make clear from the beginning that I do not keep secrets that may come up in individual communication such as telephone calls, letters, or individual visits. Since a good many couple therapies begin with visits from individuals, the therapist may take pains to provide equal time to the other spouse as well as to dispel the hint of any secrets. The individual who comes to you with the revelation that he is having an affair and then says that he wants to see you with his wife but does not want the affair revealed must be presented with several options: (1) He can break off the affair and come into therapy with his wife; (2) he can tell his wife about the affair and they can come to see you; or (3) he can seek another therapist who does not know about the affair. Participating in keeping secrets creates triangles and invariably ties a therapist's hands.

SOME COMMON PARADIGMS

There are some common paradigms or syndromes that seem to show up in all couples therapy, gay or straight, which are useful to identify in order to plan for interventions.

Pursuer-Distancer Syndrome

Commonly encountered in couples work, this syndrome comes with a predictable outcome. Basically, the pursuer-distancer idea describes a situation where one person in a relationship pursues the other, while the one pursued backpedals. The more a pursuer pursues, the more the distancer backs off. The predictable outcome? Well, first, you cannot break the pattern by pursuing more. The only way you can get a distancer in this configuration to come closer is to get the pursuer to back off. That's the *only* way. I have never seen it fail, nor have I ever seen the distancer move closer without this maneuver.

Be aware that this pursuer-distancer pattern is not fixed in a relationship—one person is not always the pursuer, while the other person is not always the distancer. (This syndrome, too, is context related.) In fact, I have seen many situations where one person starts out really pursuing the other in a relationship, while the other backs off. But sometimes when a relationship gets established and moves into another phase, the original pursuer becomes the distancer and the distancer becomes the pursuer.

By the way, this pattern is present only in some relationships and in some situations. It does not follow that if one person pursues the other person will distance and that they will develop this syndrome. Nor does it mean that if one person is distant in a relationship the other will begin to pursue.

Barry, 35, and Kyle, 26, had had an on-again/off-again

relationship for the better part of two years. Barry wanted a commitment, while Kyle was highly ambivalent. Barry, a friend, not a client, would regale me with stories about how he would almost get what he wanted from Kyle and then Kyle would emotionally flee. He was a very frustrated man. Barry would ignore my mild reminders about backing off, and he continued to pursue, with the same results. One day, someone whom Barry had had his eye on expressed interest in him, and they stated to date. Kyle was furious, and he got jealous and attentive. All of a sudden, Barry developed insight – he understood how it all operated.

Polarization

When conflict exists between two people in a relationship, you can reasonably expect some form of polarization, where one person takes one extreme on an issue and the other person takes the opposite. You see this with families, where one parent becomes stern and unbending while the other becomes almost impossibly permissive. Often, they feign agreement while continuing to undermine each other's position. This provides further ground for triangulation, especially where children are involved, but it also creates a sticking point in couples work.

Myrna was a stickler for budgets, balanced checkbooks, and financial planning. She and Elise had combined their finances during the first year of their relationship, when they moved in together. Elise seemingly had no notion of budgeting and planning. The two women would sit down and agree on how money should be spent. Then Elise would buy something on impulse and hide the expense by juggling payments or simply writing a check that would unbalance the budget. Myrna would find out and get furious. Elise, seemingly contrite, would agree not to do it again. The pattern repeated over and over again. Of course, over time Myrna became an ever more staunch advocate of strict budgeting, while Elise became more laissez-faire.

Blaming and Reframing

In the example above, blaming or negative labeling is all too often the norm in therapy and in life. All too easily could Elise get blamed for being irresponsible. A therapist might call Elise "passive-aggressive," while labeling Myrna as "obsessive-compulsive." These labels are negative frames – they put down a person's behavior as pathological while blocking reasonable solutions. After all, what can a couple do with those labels? What else but use them against each other in arguments in a blaming way!

Blaming gets you nowhere near a solution, but it almost always comes up in couples therapy. The therapist then gets called upon overtly or covertly to decide who is right. There are entire books devoted to the art of reframing, so our discussion here will remain cursory. A good place to learn more about the underpinnings of reframing is *Change* (Watzlawick, Weakland, and Fisch, 1974). The label "polarization" is a positive reframe. It implies that the normal order of things has produced a pattern where two people have moved to opposite sides on an issue, and it calls on them to come up with a solution involving equal participation. It does not imply that one person is right while the other is wrong.

Other examples of reframing: A nagging, overprotective grandma is called a concerned, perhaps too concerned, grandmother, and then is challenged to find productive ways to focus her concerns. A spouse whose behavior swings from preoccupation to overconcern and physical clumsiness around his wife is told that he has tapped into the need for more attention to boundaries in the relationship. An acting-out teen is offered a range of responses to "test" his parents' new resolve around structure – his behavior, which formerly distracted from conflicts in the system and earned him a bad reputation, is re-cast as a necessary ingredient for change.

There are many other reframing configurations, strategic and otherwise. While gathering information from couples, the therapist needs to listen for blaming and negative labels and to use his/her creativity to reframe in ways that suggest solutions to the problems that the couple brings to therapy.

SUMMARY

Basically, couples therapy is about spelling out options and helping people make choices from among those options. It sounds simple, but it is not, because in between the couple and the options are all sorts of dysfunctional sequences based on history – history of the couple, histories of the families of origin. The therapist needs to bring to bear all the knowledge he or she has accrued about where the partners should be developmentally at this point in their relationship, how they share power, what kinds of pressures work on them from church and community, and what factors are unique to them or to their situation – all just to help formulate the options in the first place. This is true for heterosexual as well as homosexual couples.

Up to this point, we have assembled the building blocks – exploring the unique problems and conditions encountered by same-sex couples, delineating a particular orientation to therapy in general and couples therapy in particular. We will now move on to the specific application of this information to the task of working with same-sex couples in an age of anxiety and discovery.

6

SOME INTERVENTIONS

Therapy with same-sex couples may begin with a variety of scenarios. Here are some possibilities.

Scenario #1

The two casually dressed men sat across from me making preliminary assessments of me and my surroundings. "Well," I began, after some small talk and a bit of joining, "what can I do for the two of you?"

"Do you want to start?" Tom asked Edward.

"Go ahead," Edward answered.

"Well," Tom sighed, "we've been together for five years, and we've been through a lot, but lately we're just not getting along. Nothing really serious. I guess we just have communication problems."

This we might term the "expected scenario"—two people in a relationship that has gotten somewhat off track. They feel that improved communication will get them back in synchrony. The particular lament about communication difficulties covers a multitude of sins. Usually teaching communication skills alone merely scratches the surface.

Scenario #2

You could cut the tension with a knife. "Jim admitted this week that he has been seeing someone else," Will snapped. "After three years together he doesn't know if he wants us to stay together. Frankly, I don't know whether we're going to survive this!"

A crisis situation. The triangle rears its ugly head. You can probably count on a healing period, if the affair ends, then possibly a ritual to close out this chapter in the relationship.

Scenario #3

"I'm glad you could make it, Sherry," I said. "When Janet came to see me last week she expressed some doubts about whether you would come in."

"Sure," Sherry replied, "but I still don't know why you wanted me here. She's the one who's depressed."

Here's a situation where one person presents with a generalized symptom, but check out the relationship! Working with the relationship should expedite your treatment of the symptom.

Scenario #4

"I love Cindy, I really do, and I really don't think we need to come to therapy, but she insisted. We can work this out, I know we can! Can't we, Cindy? (pause) Cindy??!"

It is not unusual for couples to come into therapy with one of them having already decided to end the relationship. The therapy is seen as a "safe haven" for leaving the soon-to-be-jilted partner.

Scenario #5

"You asked me over the phone to bring him in, too. Henry is my lover, and I have AIDS."

We will devote an entire chapter to AIDS, so we will not address the issues here (see Chapter 8).

Of course, there are other initial scenarios in therapy, but these present over and over again in heterosexual as well as

homosexual couples. Although the presenting complaints
may be similar, the underlying struggles may be quite different. In fact, I am often asked about what kinds of problems
same-sex couples present with – whether they are the same
or different from heterosexual couple issues. For the most
part I would say that the presenting issues are often (not
always) very similar. Obviously, though, many of the issues
we have already discussed put unique pressures on same-sex
couples. The astute, informed therapist can pick up relatively soon on whether these unique pressures alone are acting
on the relationship, whether the issues involve the same
stuff that all couples face, or whether there is an interaction
between the two. The last possibility is the most common.

As the initial session or sessions unfold, the therapist
takes note of pertinent data: gender, individual ages (life
cycle issues), age of relationship (life cycle issues), money
and power issues, race/religion, issues of differentiation from
each other and from family of origin, use of substances, sexual compatibility/problems, rules about outside sex versus
monogamy, jobs and job pressures, individual friends and
couple friends, boundaries, cutoffs, recurring unproductive
sequences, blaming, polarizations, and feelings for each other.

Please note that I do not wish to underplay the importance of feelings between two people. The issue of how one
feels often determines the course of a relationship. However,
there is no single therapeutic technique as overused and
overemphasized as the exploration of feelings. Such exploration may continue *ad nauseum* in therapy without any real
change taking place for the couple. The lack of resolution of
other issues in therapy can have a real effect on how people
perceive that they feel about each other. And other pressing
issues may hamper any attempt at expression of feelings.

In planning for this chapter I have become acutely aware
of the difficulties of describing the therapy process in the
abstract. Every therapist assembles information on an internal map that taps into the clients' belief systems in a way
that initiates change. Since the implementation of change is
part science and part art, idiosyncratic patterns of operation
are certain to creep into the therapy. Rather than try to

analyze my idiosyncrasies as a therapist, I think it best to rely on some actual case studies, from which the reader can make a determination about the general scheme of therapy and then decide how he/she might apply his/her own creativity to a particular situation.

I have chosen not to present session-by-session case studies, because I want to avoid a "cookbook" approach to doing therapy. These case studies will highlight some important issues without presenting the individual exchanges.

SOME CASE EXAMPLES

Paul and George

Let's start with an easy one. Paul, 40, and George, 33, came into therapy seven years into their relationship. They both agreed that the last six months had been very difficult for them. Both were articulate, verbal, middle-class white men. George had thinning hair and almost looked to be the senior of the two. They had bought a home together several years ago, which they continued to share.

George complained of a lack of physical expressiveness on Paul's part and described a brief flirtation that his partner had had six months before. Despite the nonsexual nature of this flirtation, George was still clearly hurt by it.

As the session continued, George described his extreme investment in the relationship from the start. He was 26, Paul 33, when they met, and Paul seemed so much older, so settled, so mature. Back then, Paul had already owned his own business for five years. So, George said, he had become almost an extension of Paul. He had no friends of his own, no separate activities, other than work. It had only been in the last six months that he had begun to emerge as a separate person, to feel as if he had real worth on his own.

A large part of George's new awareness had to do with a burgeoning career in sales. During the last year he had begun to really establish himself as a "success." His income had caught up with and passed Paul's. On the other hand, Paul, who had just turned 40, was in the midst of trying to decide

whether or not to sell his business and try his hand at something else — what he did not know.

They both described a minimal social life with other couples and few individual friends. They both felt that their
families were accepting of their relationship (but subsequent
genograms showed extreme cutoffs in both families of origin).

Both men were HIV+, but remained healthy, with adequate T4 counts. George was not happy with the frequency
of their sex life, while Paul felt it was adequate. Both seemed
eager to get the relationship back on track.

Some obvious issues emerge from these initial data. First
is a gender-related issue: two men living together, with issues of competition and compatibility, striking an initial balance based on elements that have changed over the course of
years. Next are obvious life-cycle issues: the individual issues of adulthood and midlife dilemma; the issues of a couple
together for seven years (yes, the seven-year itch really does
exist).

I mention the gender issue first because there are real
differences between how two men handle competition and
compatibility in a relationship and how it is done by a man
and a woman or by two women. As we discussed earlier, men
are much more conscious of disparities in income and status,
and they are much more likely to compete for superiority or
to attune themselves to their inequalities. In this situation,
George had clearly seen himself as subordinate for the greater part of the relationship, but now his new found career
status had him questioning his old role. Also, as these men
get older the seven-year age difference in actuality becomes
less significant as a factor in their relationship, but the mem-
ories linger on. So old patterns of relating, while no longer
really helpful, may continue. The therapist in this situation
needs to help the couple establish new ways of relating that
avoid the old assumptions.

Finally, these factors have combined with cutoffs from
families of origin to create an enmeshed relationship, a two-
against-the-world stance, not unheard of in opposite-sex couples but much more common in same-sex liaisons.

This therapy was brief, the recommendations reasonably simple: permission to seek separate outside activities, linkage with some other couples, and some sex-and-affection exercises adapted from Bernie Zilbergeld's *Male Sexuality* (that also helped heal the hurt from the recent flirtation). Some longer-term suggestions were also made concerning family-of-origin cutoffs. Sometimes couples in this situation need permission to have alternative activities and to develop individual friendships. With male couples, you need to be clear that your prescription means nonsexual outside activities (I never *prescribe* outside sex as a solution to anything, but neither do I condemn it if it works in a relationship). The couple socializing obviously is an easier prescription in a large urban area, where couples have access to each other through organizations or friends.

The sex exercises were included for two reasons. First, the men had some dissatisfaction with their sex life. Second, if one person feels neglected in a relationship (both did in this situation), then it won't do just to recommend outside activities. Nor will the sex exercises alone work in the face of enmeshment. The sex exercises give them a chance to focus on each other in an intimate way, while separate activities allow them to experience the separateness they need at this point in their relationship, as well as enabling them to bring more stimulation into their coupled life.

The genogram work with these two was designed to expand the possibilities for the future. The continuation of emotional cutoffs can seriously inhibit relationship potential. Reconnecting people to families of origin or accepting that reconnection is impossible and providing some alternatives enhances options for the future.

Peter and Ken

Peter, 32, and Ken, 27, presented with some of the same issues as George and Paul, but underlying problems dictated an entirely different course in therapy.

These two men had lived together for one year and defined themselves as a couple for two years. Ken, the younger, had recently seen his career take hold. He traveled as a computer systems consultant. During the last year he had operated on a schedule that had him gone just about every week from Monday through Friday as well as some weekends. Clearly, he had recently begun to feel his own power as he experienced success in his work. On the surface he had never behaved as if he were dependent on Peter and Peter had not pushed his maturity and financial superiority in any way.

Peter liked domesticity. He was a nest-builder. He liked predictability, the comfort of home and spouse, and, while not a stodgy person, he liked order and predictability. He had lived in the same apartment for eight years; Ken's moving-in had represented a real change for him. Peter had a master's degree in education, taught high school, and felt financially comfortable.

Peter and Ken had met on the rebound; both had been in relationships of between one and two years before they met. Both relationships had ended badly, and they were both figuratively still licking their wounds when friends had introduced them.

Here's what they described to me: They were unresolved about the monogamy issue – Peter wanted monogamy, while Ken said he was unsure (he was evasive about how he was operating at the present time). Peter was jealous about their time together – he wanted more time together and more sex together – while Ken wanted more space. Peter put the relationship first, then his job, while Ken put job first, then relationship. Peter was ready for the two of them to buy a house together, while Ken backed away from that commitment. They had few couple friends, and both said that they did little with friends individually when they were both in town. Peter only saw his friends when Ken was away. Ken had friends in various cities whom he saw while on the road. Peter was not so sure that the people Ken saw on the road were only friends.

During the next several sessions several other important issues emerged. Genograms showed that Peter came from an "Ozzie and Harriet" kind of family: intact, traditional, supportive, suburban. Ken came from a divorced family. His mother struggled alone with three children for several years, then she remarried and the family moved many times in the next 10 years. Ken had only recently reconnected with his natural father, with whom he had maintained a very strained and distant relationship through the years. For Ken, whose family did not know he was gay, there were obvious emotional cutoffs to resolve.

Ken also began to distance in the therapy sessions. By the third session he had decided to move out of Peter's apartment and to find his own space. At that point, the therapy had magnified the extent of the issues with which this couple was dealing. The very nature of the therapy process will sometimes add to the pressure a couple is experiencing. Despite steps to point out this process and to decrease the pressure on Ken, he announced that he wanted out of the relationship just a few sessions later.

During the next year, Ken and Peter made several abortive attempts to reconcile. As soon as they would settle into their relationship, Ken would bolt. It later became evident that Ken had maintained several clandestine affairs in other cities. Ken was not "at fault." He fits the description of what Charles Silverstein (1981) calls the "thrill-seeker," while Peter could be described as the "nest-builder." Together they are not a good fit. Together they have the potential to aggravate each other's normal inclinations, driving one another to polarized positions. The thrill-seeker, with his penchant for many sexual partners and adventure, feels very constrained by the limits of the well-constructed nest. The nest-builder feels wronged and insecure around someone who doesn't want to help to line the nest and may try to nest even more elaborately.

With this couple I tried some therapeutic maneuvers to see whether some kind of good fit might result. I suggested that Peter back off on the mutual home-buying idea. I gave Ken some assignments concerning the reconnection with his father and stepmother. I prescribed some separate tasks with friends, even when each one was in town. I also suggested that perhaps Ken really needed to feel separate in the relationship before he could make a further commitment. They both initially cooperated with these moves; however, other issues got in the way.

The tip-off really came early in the lack of real agreement about monogamy versus outside sex (I avoid the term "promiscuity" because it has judgmental overtones). Also, the two men had very different priorities at this point in their lives. They were at a time in the life cycle of a relationship when each member gets called upon to consider the next step in the commitment, when the "new" has worn off. Ken was really focused on his career, to the exclusion of almost everything else. Peter was unable to look beyond the marriage convention, the belief that living together demonstrates a real form of commitment. Ken's dishonesty concerning his "affairs" provided the final blow.

I saw both men individually, each several times during the year following couples work. Peter bought a home on his own and gathered his friends around him. Ken went on to another short-term relationship and continued an intense involvement with his career. They did not maintain a friendship with each other.

Lori and Janine

Lori and Janine presented a somewhat different picture from what I was used to seeing. They were mental health center clients, very much semi-rural, working-class women. Both were in their late twenties. Unlike other lesbian couples I have seen, their relationship just "kind of happened." They met, became friends, and eventually became sexual with each other. They did so without road maps. They had no lesbian friends. Neither had experienced a lesbian social scene. They were not familiar with women's organizations. Nor did they read books that might have familiarized them with other options for their lives. In Southern parlance, they were "just plain folks," who happened to have hit an unexpected, confusing snag or two along the way.

Both worked blue-collar jobs around blue-collar men. Lori ran a parts counter for a local auto parts store. Janine worked an assembly line in a fan belt factory. They came in for some guidance because, after two years together, neither knew exactly where they were going. Was this just a temporary arrangement until the right man came along? Each one knew that she was not really interested in men. Was this the beginning of a long-term relationship? Neither one knew what that meant, especially in this context. Neither one was articulate about these concerns, but the gist of the issue was clear.

When they came in they were both afraid – afraid of being discovered by friends and family, afraid of telling anyone, afraid of what all this meant. They were also highly suspicious of this Yankee shrink who sat with them, asked questions and listened. They really didn't know what they wanted from me, and for about fifty cents they would have gotten up and run out, if I had told them that that was okay to do.

This is the kind of couple that you probably will not see more than a time or two your first go-around. They need to find some support and a few answers without being overwhelmed. They probably experience some negative feelings about people who go to shrinks in the first place. They can easily be overwhelmed by the therapy situation and an overabundance of material heaped on them by a well-meaning therapist, eager to be helpful. You need to slip into a semicrisis mode and give them some things to pursue that they can handle a bit at a time and at their own speed. Intermingling some reassurance is helpful.

With Lori and Janine, I listened some, asked some questions that were not too threatening, and assumed a posture that said, "You are not crazy; you are experiencing a problem that other women have experienced and resolved, and I want you to talk to some of them." I gave them several resources: a support group, a woman's bookstore, a social organization. I agreed to see them another time and to be available if they wanted to make additional appointments at some time in the future, but I emphasized that their situation was more normal than they thought and that they could expect some relief.

Cassie and Delores

Educated, sophisticated, highly conversant with the up-per-middle-class lesbian world—this describes both Cassie, 34, and Delores, 29. Cassie was a physician with the beginnings of a very successful ophthalmology practice. Delores taught mathematics in a private secondary school. Both women had been in one other lesbian relationship, lasting a year or two each.

The two of them clearly were not doing well together—no dramatic fights or outside affairs, just a general malaise. The two of them had defined themselves as a couple for two-and-a-half years. They had never lived together, but they stayed together three or four nights per week, almost always at Cassie's house. Delores was very sensitive about any invasion of her space, and she did not really welcome any encroachment, even from an intimate. The struggle around this seemingly minor issue had intensified recently, as Cassie planned some major renovation of her home. Delores still resisted a temporary resettlement at her place during the renovation period.

Obviously this conflict had more significance than met the eye. It had to do with commitment. The clues came from two areas: the developmental stage of their relationship and family-of-origin issues.

Many relationships manage to survive the first several years. After that the reality of commitment begins to intrude. The proverbial phrase, "The honeymoon is over," has some real meaning. Some couples can survive the ensuing changes; some cannot. Mattison and McWhirter (1984, p. 16), writing about male couples, describe years two and three of a relationship as the Nesting Stage. They characterize this stage as dealing with issues of homemaking, the search for compatibility, a decline of what they call limerance (the magic feeling that goes with the early phases of a relationship), and ambivalence as commitment begins to play a larger role.

These issues had real meaning for Cassie and Delores. Cassie seemed ready to make the jump to a committed, life-long relationship, while Delores seemed confused and unwilling to commit herself past a certain point. However, even she sensed that something had to change, that they could not just keep going on as they had.

In the meantime, family-of-origin pressures contributed to the situation. Cassie, an oldest child, lived almost 1,500 miles from her parents and siblings. Even though geographical distance does not necessarily equate with emotional distance, Cassie used the distance to help avoid dealing with her family about her lifestyle. In some ways, she seemed ready to begin to deal with them, but she wanted to know that she had a partner who would support her through the process. Delores' family lived locally. She had one sister, who was also lesbian, but her parents did not know about the sexual orientation of either daughter. Delores did not feel comfortable enough with her sexual orientation or with her relationship in general to risk taking a stand with them around this relationship.

It took eight or ten sessions for her to realize that she couldn't really make a commitment to this relationship or to any lesbian relationship at this time. Issues of separation needed to be addressed. Parting ways officially took place several months after we had finished therapy.

As a follow-up, Delores began to see men shortly after they finished therapy. She eventually got married but was divorced after one year. Cassie met another woman about a year later, and they have shared a life together for the last three years. Cassie has come out to her parents, who have really struggled with her homosexuality. She has remained firm with them and clear about her lifestyle.

This relationship responded to internal and external pressures about the readiness for commitment. It was not that either woman was "more together" than the other, but that normal issues of commitment were compounded by issues unique to same-sex couples.

Harry and Lloyd

Harry and Lloyd did not start out in couples counseling together. Harry came in to see me with complaints of general malaise, anxiety, mild depression. He also complained of "parent trouble." His parents, he said, would not leave him alone. It seems that two years before he told them that he was gay. That was when he and Lloyd had begun living together, while they both attended graduate school. They had been coupled for two years before that, but had attended schools several hundred miles apart. Then they saw each other on weekends and during school breaks.

Harry's parents had been furious when he told them. They had insisted that their 23-year-old son stop seeing this other person or they would withdraw all financial support for graduate school. Harry refused, and they made good on their threat. After one quarter of trying to get by on loans, Harry told his parents that he had broken things off with Lloyd. In actuality, the two men continued living together and maintained their relationship.

The money flowed to Harry, once again, but this meant that Lloyd could never answer the telephone in his own apartment. It also meant that, when Harry's parents visited twice a year or so, Lloyd had to find someplace else to stay. Despite the subterfuge, the two men finished graduate school and moved to the city together. Lloyd still didn't answer his own telephone.

Money remained an obstacle to freedom for Harry. His parents were very wealthy, and he was a struggling writer. They had hinted that if he ever again decided to be "that way," they would disinherit him once and for all. His sister had assured him that they meant it!

Lloyd had been absent almost two months at the time of Harry's visit. His father had suffered a heart attack, and the family had insisted that only Lloyd could keep the family business going in his father's absence. His family knew all about Harry and their relationship, although his sexual orientation was not openly discussed. Neither Lloyd nor his family had mentioned Harry in light of the family crisis.

So Lloyd quit his job (which he hadn't much cared for anyway) and went north to deal with the crisis. He and Harry had seen each other over one weekend since then.

Psychiatrist Murray Bowen has made the observation that when coupling, people tend to seek partners who are at the same level of differentiation from their familes of origin. I do not know whether I buy this universally, but it certainly fit in this situation. Not only did the families violate the boundaries of this couple, but both men went along with almost no protest. In Bowen terms, they showed a lack of differentiation from their families of origin.

Several months later, when I finally saw the two of them together, the caring was obvious. They both cared about each other deeply and seemed genuinely supportive of each other. The relationship had experienced rough spots through the years in predictable areas — a brief affair, a financial crisis, etc. Still, the fabric of the relationship remained sturdy.

I had already begun to do some family-of-origin work with Lloyd by getting him to connect with a brother and an aunt, who both knew of his sexual orientation. Together we explored what Harry and Lloyd could reasonably expect from each other, as well as what they could and should demand from the world. I was candid with them about what I saw as boundary issues between them as a couple and their families. Lloyd and I also began to look at some family-of-origin issues, and he was successful in getting his married brother to take over some of the responsibilities for his ailing parents.

Harry settled into a business of his own, and Lloyd made a complete career change during the ensuing years. I saw them as a couple over four or five years, but still only with widely-spaced visits or clusters of visits as they hit some rough spots. It took a number of years for Harry to really deal honestly with his parents, who have yet to disown him, although, they are not pleased with his lifestyle. When he finally did come out to them, he had real support from friends and other family members, as well as from Lloyd.

SUMMARY

In this chapter we have met five couples who presented with different "run-of-the-mill" kinds of problems. Our first couple presented with a problem characterized by a shift in roles and perceptions within the relationship as a product of time and maturity. The second couple offered an example of "a bad fit" based on different needs for closeness and distance and different ideas about what life should hold for them. The third couple needed a road map. The fourth couple struggled with differing acceptance levels of their sexual feelings. The fifth couple presented with issues that primarily called for looking beyond the functioning of the dyad and focusing on family-of-origin issues.

I have called these five situations run-of-the-mill because they represent the kinds of cases one might see in private practice or in an agency setting, and they do not require the specialized knowledge that a therapist might need with domestic violence, severe substance abuse, or the effects of ravaging illness. In the next three chapters, we will look at situations requiring a more specific, specialized knowledge and focus.

7

PARENTING/BLENDED
FAMILY ISSUES

Gay parents face the same parenting issues as their heterosexual counterparts. However, straight parents do *not* face all the same issues as their homosexual counterparts.

When a gay parent brings a new partner into the home or brings a child into an already existing household, he or she will confront all the same issues of blended family that heterosexual parents will face.

Since this book is dealing with couples, we will skip over the issues confronting gay/lesbian single parents. And since several good books have been written about blended family issues for heterosexual families, we will concentrate here on the issues that are different for same-sex couples, stepparents, and their children.

I'll start by answering a question that people think of but generally do not ask. No, children raised in gay households do not have a greater chance of turning out gay. No evidence exists that a gay or lesbian couple or a gay or lesbian individual raising a child will influence the child's sexual orientation any more than will a heterosexual environment. After all, most gay men and women are the products of heterosexual upbringing. The fact that this question exists at all in people's minds represents the first major difference that same-sex parents contend with that opposite-sex parents do not.

I make the assumption that for all couples adding a child to a household increases the complexity of things. Now some might argue that a child increases the bonding between natural parents, and I will not quibble with that. And there are those who might say that adding a child makes it easier for some families to sort out roles, and I do not want to argue that point either (even though many couples get triangulated through children). Still, on a day-to-day basis, adding a dependent being to a household increases the operating complexity of that system.

I generally tell families with whom I am working that there are three components that the family must deal with: (1) the individual and his/her needs; (2) the couple and its needs; and (3) the family and its needs. Which of these components do you suppose commonly gets neglected first? The correct answer is (2). Yes, under pressure the needs of a couple in family life usually drop out first. Why? Just because people go to work to support themselves and their families and have "individual" experiences. And then they come home and have to deal with the needs of dependents, so they have "family" experiences. Often they find that there is little or no time left for purely couple experiences. Or, at least, that is the way things are perceived.

Well, there are several misconceptions in those perceptions. First of all, work experience alone may or may not provide adequate individual experience. Second, taking care of the everyday needs of the family usually doesn't provide really satisfying family time. And third, ignoring couple functions will likely cost you somewhere down the road.

It's not hopeless. It just requires some organization that many couples, particularly male couples, are not especially good at. Men, after all, still do not take a primary child-caretaking role in our culture; in fact, in most families where men contribute to childcare, it is under the direction of women. For coupled women, culturally well-versed in child-rearing, competition about the "right way" to raise the child or children may become more of an issue than it does for men.

DIFFERENT PARENTING CONFIGURATIONS

Same-sex couples may be involved with children in a variety of ways—as parents, prospective parents, or non-active fathers or mothers.

Cutoffs

The partial or total cutoff is not uncommon. Some gay parents have either been forced or have chosen to have little contact or no contact with their children. One friend of mine, for example, is forbidden to see his children for longer than two hours twice per year without the other parent being present. Courts usually go to this extreme only when dealing with child molesters or physically abusive parents. He is neither (a possibility that the court seems to have ignored), which demonstrates another instance of prejudice against gay parents.

Other parents, in their eagerness to experience the gay life after years of acting straight, completely surrender the vestiges of their former lives, including their children. Some parents simply distance from lack of interest, unwillingness to provide financial support, or compliance with the request of their former spouse. Sometimes the separation process has involved bitterness, recrimination, accusations, and admonitions. The divorcing couple may feel that distance is the only way to allow the wound to heal. It is not unusual for the non-gay parent to feel furious and manipulated and lied to. Sometimes the former spouse insists that contact with the child be minimal or nonexistent as a condition for the divorce or separation. It also gives the "deserted" spouse some feeling of control in a difficult situation.

The issue of the departing parent's sexual orientation also comes into play as a secret. The straight parent often does not want children, family, or friends to know the real reason for the divorce. And, once again, there is fear that informing a child may bias the child toward becoming gay.

By the way, it is usually the parents' anxieties that make

this revelation or discovery traumatic. Many children, even young ones, handle the information fairly comfortably when the parents do the same. Also, it is worth mentioning that there are some couples who work together on winding up the marriage phase of the relationship and who successfully forge an ongoing friendship based on their years together and the parenting responsibilities that they will continue to share. (This is a goal to be worked towards with heterosexual couples.)

What about the effects of this cutoff process on the new homosexual couple? Even when one or both members of a couple appear cutoff from their offspring or when contact is minimal, the fact of having produced children and not hav-ing contact with them becomes an issue in therapy. The partners may assure you that they do not wish contact with a child or children, but the issue may run more deeply than they suppose. Simply as a cutoff it can affect some intimacy issues for the couple. The nonparental member might, for example, fear that he or she will be abandoned, just as the partner abandoned the children. The potential stepparent, who has never had children, may push for contact in order to satisfy his or her own parental fantasies. In the meantime, a custodial ex-spouse with no wish to instigate contact may provide fodder for a triangle between curious partner, recal-citrant ex-spouse, and biological parent.

Voluntary or semi-voluntary cutoffs from children occur more frequently for male couples than for female. Our social attitudes, court system, and familial expectations all tend to support the role of mother as custodial parent.

A growing number of same-sex couples have regular con-tact with the biological children of one or both of the part-ners. For those men and women there are basically three scenarios: (1) visitation on some sort of regular or sporadic basis; (2) informal custody, where a parent mostly raises the child without legal support; and (3) formal custody, where the parent has legal custody and claim.

Visitation

Visitation with a noncustodial parent has become more and more common in this era of escalating divorce rates. In many ways, this fact makes visitation issues easier to deal with, since many more children now experience the shuttle between parents' homes. A child's explanation, "I'll be at my father's this weekend," seldom prompts raised eyebrows. However, the question, "What is your stepmother like?" is almost sure to create awkwardness for the child of a gay, coupled parent.

Predictably, there are certain potential issues for children and their families with visitation arrangements. First, just the transition itself creates tension and confusion, especially for the younger child. The physical arrangement of the houses, the rules, the sleeping quarters, the neighborhoods, playmates, travel arrangements – all need to be sorted out. These changes may prove more disorganizing for children than adults understand, and it is not unusual to see acting-out problems just before and just after a visitation period. (Some parents choose to pick up and drop off their children at neutral places like restaurants or school in order to minimize the abruptness of the transition.)

Secrets spawn triangles, and in most divorce/recoupling situations there is, at the very least, a built-in curiosity factor. Sometimes things go well beyond simple curiosity. Children returning from a weekend visit often hear, "So what did you do this weekend at your father's?" This seemingly innocent question often hides a plethora of agendas, and the child easily, sometimes willingly, gets caught up in the triangle.

For the parents, too, there is tension. Many same-sex couples are not prepared to deal honestly with their relationship. They change sleeping arrangements when the child arrives. They watch their use of pronouns – "we" is avoided if it implies anything other than friendship. They pretend a lot. All of these things and more upset the regular routine of the household. The biological parent may begin to feel like a juggler, while the non-parent, who has no experience with children, does not really understand all the games that are going on. She may also feel abruptly neglected, as her partner creates more distance for the sake of the child, as well as for the sake of preserving certain illusions. Sometimes this situation creates major barriers for the couple.

Donna, 37, and Lisa, 33, had lived together for almost five years. Donna, previously married to Jason, had two children, Adam, 13, and David, 11, whose custody she had given up in order to facilitate her divorce. Jason and his parents, who were helping to raise the children, were fundamentalist Christians, presumably with no knowledge of Donna's sexual preference. Donna enjoyed liberal visitation rights, which she feared she would lose if Jason or his parents discovered her homosexuality. The natural curiosity of her two boys just entering adolescence increased the chances of discovery. She was finding it ever more difficult to sustain the pretense that she and Lisa were only roommates. As an adult, Lisa had never considered a heterosexual marriage and family life, but when she fell in love with Donna she began entertaining intense fantasies of being a stepmother or "aunt" to the boys. She welcomed the children's visits and enthusiastically planned activities for them to do as a family.

The couple sought therapy because of an escalating pattern of angry quarrels, which exploded almost immediately before and after the boys' visits. Donna complained that Lisa was intrusive, while Lisa felt pushed away and ignored. Donna did not want Lisa included in the family, feeling that she had too much to lose if their relationship were revealed.

We worked on Lisa's fantasies about being part of Donna's family, and I encouraged her to develop more separate activities when the boys were present. Still, the difficulties of the situation posed some very real limits on their potential in therapy and contributed to the couple's eventual dissolution.

Orientation differences *may* also pose a problem. In this case, by orientation I mean a qualitative difference between gay men and women who have been involved in heterosexual marriages and who may or may not have produced children, on the one hand, and on the other, gay men and women who have never been involved in heterosexual marriages. Now, I say "may" because I do not have any quantitative evidence to support my speculations. But I have had a good deal of experience with married or formerly married gay men, who have cued me in to the difficulties they have dealing with gay men who have never been married. I have also questioned a number of lesbians, formerly married to men, who report the same experiences.

There is no question in my mind that our society has very strong notions about marriage roles and responsibilities. We discussed these earlier when we explored gender roles in our culture. It seems plausible that those men and women who have struggled with their sexual orientation and have chosen for a time to try to live within the confines of heterosexuality may have a built-in investment in living as "straight" a life as possible, and that this orientation continues after they have come out. For example, many of the previously married gay men I have dealt with strongly reject stereotypical gay behaviors and attitudes about the permanence of relationships. They assert that they are the same people they were when married – only their sexual behavior has refocused. Gay men who have pretty much grown up gay may exhibit a wider tolerance for many gay behaviors; yet, they may not really understand the orientation of a partner who has more interest in embracing heterosexual attitudes.

In major cities, the opportunity often exists for previously or currently married gay men and lesbians to join support groups with others who think more as they do. I have found that such support groups provide a very valuable service for these individuals and help to pave the way for more productive match-ups – in terms of friendships as well as potential romantic liaisons. Therapists should consider providing such a resource for their clients if it is not available already in their communities. (Certain difficulties may exist in recruiting men and women for these groups, but that is another subject.)

As we have seen, the visitation process for gay men and women *does* involve all the varied issues that heterosexual partners encounter, plus it places some additional demands on these couples and their children. While I am not adamant about openness with children concerning the true nature of the gay couple's relationship, I do feel that such openness is a goal that should be worked toward, at a speed that is comfortable for the parent, the child, and the family. Most often gay parents go to great lengths to protect themselves from potential repercussions from family. Sometimes the spectre of those repercussions proves quite real. Still, secrecy has so many negative implications. The belief that the infrequency of the child's visits does not make it worth dealing with the reality of the gay family may generate negative feelings in the present as well as the future. Just because the child only visits once a month or several times a year does not mean that she does not develop a sense that something is being kept from her. Obviously, secrecy in this instance breeds emotional cutoffs between parent and child. The child will eventually begin to suspect that something is up and will know that her parent is not willing to take her into his confidence. The tension that goes along with this kind of secrecy also will take its toll on the parent and her relationship with her partner.

From a clearly social perspective, the secrecy perpetuates the idea that there is something wrong with a homosexual orientation. So even though concerns are generally expressed in terms of more personal issues, you need to be aware that the secrecy will affect the individuals' and couple's perceptions of their own legitimacy and worth. When the issue of a parent's sexual orientation is handled with sensitivity, one should not expect to see adverse long-term effects on the child. When children spend time around the couple and their friends, gay and straight, and participate in the normal household routine, they generally accept the situation without too much upset.

Sometimes children make requests of a gay or lesbian parent that may seem to strain the boundaries of openness. For example, an adolescent may request that her mother drive her to a party without the partner. Or, when a father has AIDS, a child may want to tell friends that he has a more acceptable disease. Such situations need to be handled on a case-by-case basis. A client with AIDS told his daughter living in another city that it was okay with him if she told friends that he had cancer. He reasoned that, if he had custody and dealt with her friends on a regular basis, the issue might be different. But from his perspective, it was not necessary for his daughter to fight this fight when it involved the prospect of cruelty and rejection from her friends, who mostly had never met her father anyway. In this case, the father and daughter were very open with each other about the progress of his disease and how it affected his life on a daily basis.

As the example of Donna and Lisa illustrates, the parent and non-parent should be aware of each other's needs in the situation. The partners will find it valuable to discuss what they want to do as a family, what activities work best for parent and child, what will happen with couple activities during visitation, and what space might be needed for individual time. Sometimes the biological parent pushes too hard for the partner's participation, and the partner may comply just because she feels that she should. Just as a partner may openly resent being "sent away" during visitation, that partner may also resent being included in everything when there are things she would prefer to do alone. Remember, many people who do not have children are not very comfortable around them for concentrated or prolonged periods of time.

Earlier in the chapter we discussed the implications of triangles and triangulation of children in the divorce process and its aftermath. Let me reiterate that the adults in a triangular situation should not get the "blame." In fact, blaming is not useful for breaking up triangles. Children, too, often have a good deal to gain by continued involvement in a triangle. For example, an adolescent might "prefer" continued involvement in his mother and father's struggle to sort out their conflictual situation, when the alternative might be focusing on some unresolved peer conflicts at school. Playing the adults' game sometimes looks vastly less threatening. Your therapeutic solutions to nonproductive triangles need to involve all sides of the triangle, remembering that all sides find their "gains," even in what looks to the outsider to be a dysfunctional situation.

Informal Custody

Informal custody situations arise in a variety of ways. They may happen by default, when a custodial parent is unwilling or unable to handle the major parenting responsibilities. They may evolve by choice of parent or child, as a solution to an immediate problem. The may occur because of job changes or moves, etc., that were not factors when the original arrangement for custody was worked out. Whatever the reason for the informal custody situation, there is potential for uncertainty and confusion.

Mickey had three children by his marriage, Roy, 11, Sam, 8, and Cassandra, 5. He had been divorced from his wife for four years. During that time, he and Joe, his partner of three plus years had enjoyed regular alternate-week visitation from his children, who lived 150 miles distant. Sam and his mother had definite ongoing problems getting along, and Sam did a fair amount of acting out in school. In fits of exasperation, Mickey's ex-wife would insist that he take over with Sam, sometimes literally on a moment's notice. This meant a major move each time for Sam, abrupt changes in school, separation from siblings and from friends. Typically, Sam responded much better at his father's house. After several months at his father's house, he would begin to settle down. Usually it took his mother several months before she would begin to push for his return — mostly out of guilt.

These disruptions left everyone in an awkward state. Mickey wanted the best for Sam, but he felt thwarted by the on-and-off situation. Sam suffered from the repeated change. Mickey and Joe found it difficult to plan their lives together. For Mickey, intervention was awkward. His ex-wife knew about his sexual orientation, and she tolerated it as long as it was to her advantage (and she had no plans to surrender any child support). Her current husband treated Mickey with disdain. Mickey knew that she could make an ugly scene about visitation, so he hesitated to push for clearer boundaries; yet, he was acutely aware of how all of this affected Sam.

While not a common situation, this informal custody created obstacles beyond what a heterosexual couple might face for all concerned. (Mickey and Joe were not clients.) Eventually, with the help of Mickey's mother and a lot of patience, they were able to push gently for clearer boundaries. Sam's mother divorced husband number three and remarried a man who proved much more reasonable. Mickey still has only informal custody, but Sam has now lived with him steadily for two years and he continues to show improvement. Even Sam's regular visits with his mother and siblings appear to be much more productive.

Formal Custody

Formal custody adds legitimacy to what may be a highly tenuous situation. Obviously, legal custody of a child enables a parent to make decisions for the child and to have more of an impact on his/her life. Certain functions, such as permission for medical treatment, enrollment in school, etc., require legal custody, and such custody gives the family a certain stability. But custody does not always allow a parent to breathe freely. Consider the recent Georgia case of Leigh Vanderels, who lost custody of her children when the judge presiding in the divorce case learned that she was a lesbian (and then allegedly he called her employer and insisted that she be removed from her job with the county!).

Just because a gay parent has custody and raises a child does not always mean that the parent is "out" to the child. Dan raised his three children by himself for 15 years after his divorce. He never allowed himself to date or to see men until the last child went off to college. Then he came out with a vengeance and, at age 54, literally went wild in the streets. Some gay/lesbian parents persist in raising their children with the "help" of a partner, while never being explicit about the role that the partner plays in his/her life. Obviously, the physical presence of a partner raises questions that do not come up in a single-parent situation. Most gay men and lesbians raising children need the open help and support of their partners, and the children need it, too. The decision to support secrecy may put a major stress on the family relationships.

As a therapist, you will need to help gay families deal with many issues common to blended families—grandparents, in-laws, money, etc. Since we all come from unique family backgrounds, we bring different sets of perceptions about what family—blended or nuclear—should be. Grave misunderstandings can grow out of differences in these perceptions.

Sometimes a new stepparent will want to jump in eagerly to implement her parenting ideas. Sometimes the biological parent encourages it. But experience shows us that an 18-month to two-year waiting period is best before a stepparent begins to take on any real parenting responsibilities. During that time, the members of the new family need to get to know each other and to develop the trust and respect necessary for implementing successful stepparenting (assuming an authority role alone is hardly enough). Some structured setting for sharing family histories and habits with each other will prove valuable during this period. For example, perhaps the non-parent grew up in a home where you never watched TV during dinner, while the child and his mom always ate dinner in front of the TV. This situation, while not appearing on the surface to be a major one, has the potential to erupt in conflict if it goes unprocessed. Understanding differences and dealing with them openly can help the family members come up with some compromise positions that alleviate stress and tension between members.

The biological parent comes to the same-sex couple with some parental experience, ranging from very little to extensive. Often the partner comes into the relationship with no children of his/her own and consequently no parental experience (in the days of large extended families, one could get the experience without having biological children). Furthermore, the non-parent may have had no experience living with children, child-proofing the house, sharing resources with a non-adult, etc. Finding himself/herself in such a setting may provide for a rude awakening! A therapist conversant with these kinds of issues can help with the adjustment.

Blended family issues vary with many factors, not the least of which are the number of children and their ages. The demands made by a very young child are quite different from those made by an adolescent. Our task here is not to explore each developmental stage but to look at factors peculiar to gay families with permanent custody of one or more children. Still, the therapist needs to take into account developmental factors in working with these families, just as one would with any family seeking therapy.

Most families with children seek out a network of friends with children who are roughly the same age as their own. Usually this network development happens informally, although with urban patterns of job transfer, changing residences, and lack of available extended family, some families seek such a support network systematically through neighborhood organizations, churches and other friends. (I was amused and somewhat gratified recently by a public service announcement seeking to bring together mothers with children for the sake of support—such networks used to occur naturally in neighborhoods!) These networks are useful for support, commiseration, social activities, babysitters, etc. They help the family to maintain a certain level of functioning.

Most gay families have to work longer and harder to develop such networks. Sometimes they are just not available.

Furthermore, many of the organizations that might help with network development or whose presence might put the family in touch with others are simply not accessible to gay families. This can create a hardship for adults and children alike. Women do better on this score. They have more socialization experience in this area, and outsiders seem to express less concern about two women living together raising a child than they do about two men in the same circumstances.

Even friends and neighbors may not provide much support for the gay family. Neighbors may be curious, suspicious, or downright hostile. Easy interactions with neighbors, if they do occur, may take much more time to develop than for heterosexual families. This fact also places specific limitations on the children. Wanting a friend to spend the night can turn into a real crisis; neighbors' rejection may be intended for the same-sex parent rather than the child, but the child may not be able to sort out this subtlety.

Since the number of gay men and lesbians raising children is not large, most friends will be childless couples or individuals, unless the couple is fortunate enough to find heterosexual families who make no distinctions about their situations (or unless the gay family has access to other gay families). Often those heterosexual families who tolerate the situation do so only for the sake of their children, as long as no one raises the question of sexuality. Single or coupled lesbians and gay men without children generally are not attuned to a lifestyle that involves childrearing. Their homes, interests, and sympathies are not congruent with the living patterns of gay families, especially when younger children are involved.

School may provide another impediment for the gay family. Logistics may dictate that a lover pick up and deliver his stepchild to school. Who is this mysterious man, who obviously has a relationship with this child? Teachers may prove no more tolerant or informed than neighbors about the issues of homosexuality. Parent-teacher conferences can be handled by a biological parent only, but the stepparent may rightfully feel left out. Stepparents who are involved in the raising of children often like to be present at school plays, football games, career night, etc. The presence of a same-sex stepparent at such events can do a lot more than raise eyebrows. Children experience the pressure from peers, who demand to know about "that other person." Children can be notoriously cruel in their comments, especially when they sense that there may be some truth to their allegations!

So what is the best help available for families struggling with some or all of these hurdles? Networking! Networking is a key element in developing the necessary supports. Formal networking procedures may demand that the therapist step outside of comfortable, traditional therapy roles. Networking usually means starting small with the couple or the family and adding a person or two at a time to meetings that are best handled in the home or the community (to help avoid stigma about pathology). The culmination of effective networking involves a meeting with family, friends, business associates, school personnel, etc., to cover issues of concern and to make direct assignments for help from network members (for example, who will handle babysitting in an emergency.) If this sounds like an ambitious task, it is, but there is no denying the results. Of course, many families will not initially agree to such exposure. With them, the therapist needs to work slowly and to limit outside involvement to what they can handle with comfort.

Sooner or later the issue of sleeping arrangements and sex will come up. Questions about affection and sexuality are answered most easily when the couple has been appropriately open about commitments. An atmosphere of secrecy promotes trauma. I must say, though, that I have never personally seen a full-blown crisis develop when a child living with gay parents "discovers" that they are lovers. Parents and other adults, yes. Children, no. Most often children get their judgmental attitudes from adults; when they are not exposed to these judgments they seem to do quite well for themselves!

A child's questions about sex should be answered as directly and straightforwardly as possible, given the age of the child. Specific questions about "what do you do in bed?" are generally just as inappropriate in this situation as they would be if asked of heterosexual parents. The important facts are that the partners are committed to each other and that sexual expression is part of that commitment. Elaboration about sexual practices in general remains up to the couple.

CONCLUSIONS

Full-time parenting is never easy. Add a few obstacles and the difficulty expands greatly. Frankly, I can think of no advantages that a gay family has over straight counterparts. But then, gay parents often do not have the choice about assuming parental responsibilities. Besides, the same joys accrue to gay parents as to straight parents. Even though the task may not be easy, most of us feel that the investment in time and energy is justified.

As a therapist, you may find yourself limited in terms of possible solutions to gay parenting problems. Networking holds out the most promise. We will probably see a gradually increasing number of lesbians and gay men who take on the parenting role. A growing number of lesbian couples, for example, choose pregnancy through a donor to have "their own" children. Joint participation in the pregnancy does not obviate all the issues described in this chapter. Nevertheless, as acceptance of gay parenting grows, so will the chances of gay families sharing the same rewarding, productive experiences available to heterosexual families.

8

THE ISSUE OF AIDS

Acquired immune deficiency syndrome (AIDS) has ravaged the gay male population while leaving the lesbian population virtually untouched physically. For more than five years now, no topic has dominated gay male consciousness like the subject of AIDS. In major metropolitan areas, most gay males have experienced loss related to AIDS, ranging from partners to casual acquaintances to the "guy who tended bar." In more rural areas, losses may not be as apparent, but the fear still exists.

There is no question that the existence of this disease has changed people's lives. Sexual practices have changed for large numbers of people (but not for all). Many have been forced to deal with family and community in ways they assumed they could avoid. Jobs and careers have been disrupted. Some supports have disappeared while, for some, new ones have emerged. Homophobia has mushroomed in some quarters while diminishing in others. Young people have been forced to deal with death and dying, struggling with situations reminiscent of wartime or the world of the elderly — infirmity, suffering, isolation, helplessness, and loss. This may sound overly dramatic; let me assure you that it is not.

All of this continues to have an impact on the coupling process as well as on relationships that have existed over time. Obviously the effects of the disease are physical as well as emotional, and we need to begin with a general orientation to the disease itself. In this chapter, we will first look at the disease itself and how it affects the individual physically and emotionally. Then we will examine the effects on family. Finally we will look at couple issues in terms of internal pressures, external pressures, and interventions that can maximize a couple's well-being.

THE GAY MALE PWA

The orientation that we will take in this chapter pertains to the gay male population. Please do not assume that the material presented here generalizes to all persons with AIDS (PWAs). Some does; some does not. For example, we know from experience that many gay males experience cutoffs from their families of origin and may be described as disengaged from family. Stanton and Todd's (1982) work with IV drug abusers indicates that they are often very *enmeshed* with their families of origin, that often they live within blocks of their families of origin and are in daily contact with them. This difference might dictate different approaches to these two populations. On the other hand, the struggles around anxieties associated with the disease may be similar.

A good deal of written material exists on the physical/medical aspects of AIDS, so we will stick to mostly nonmedical aspects here. Still, the therapist working with same-sex male couples needs to have a basic understanding of the disease, its "phases," and the measures that people may take in order to stay as healthy as possible. Let's begin by considering the various phases of the disease, in terms of what is commonly perceived as its progression.

HIV Positive

First we have the exposure phase, when people may describe themselves as "HIV positive." This may tell all or just part of the story. Someone who tests HIV+ may remain simply HIV+ for a long period of time. No one knows just how long, but often many years. (In the early years, predictions had it that only 15% of those with HIV+ status would go on to develop full-blown AIDS. Now predictions range from 95 to 100%.) During that time, the HIV+ person may have no symptoms at all or relatively minor ones like dry, flaky skin, minor chronic cough, or symptoms easily attributed to other causes. In fact, unless tested, the HIV+ individual may have no idea that he has been exposed. Some people, it appears, may progress quite rapidly from exposure to severe illness. So far, no one has developed a measure of prediction, except to say "on the average." Most gay males in metropolitan areas either know or have heard about people whose experiences do not fit within the average.

So a hallmark for many during this HIV+ phase is fear of the unknown. "Like walking around with a time bomb inside of you that may go off at any time," many have said. The person may appear perfectly healthy on the outside, and for all practical purposes he is, but he may feel that his situation could change drastically on short notice, and for all practical purposes, it could. There are medical bench marks in current use that may give people some idea about their medical status, such as T-helper cell counts or P24 antigen levels measuring viral activity. However, once again, there are notable exceptions that test the veracity of these measures.

Generally, a T-helper cell count of 400 or higher is interpreted as some reassurance that the immune system still functions in the "normal range"; yet some people have developed full-blown AIDS with counts well above 400. Others with T-helper cell counts under 50 may stay relatively healthy and not even carry an AIDS diagnosis.

ARC

ARC stands for AIDS-related condition or complex. The person diagnosed with ARC (a PWARC) has shown some symptoms that do not "qualify" him for a diagnosis of AIDS according to Center for Disease Control (CDC) criteria. Symptoms may include things such as chronically swollen lymph nodes (lymphadenopathy), chronic fatigue, or unexplained weight loss. People may remain in this state for long periods of time without experiencing really serious, life-threatening illness, or they may progress rapidly downhill. Several people whom I have known only received the AIDS diagnosis on their deathbeds.

AIDS

When a person has experienced any infection on the CDC list of AIDS criteria, then he receives the AIDS diagnosis. This may be important for some PWAs because certain treatments may be available only to those people with the AIDS diagnosis, and some insurance companies may pay for certain treatments only with an ARC or an AIDS diagnosis. PWAs also may experience a minor version of an AIDS opportunistic infection, get diagnosed, and then go on asymptomatically for a considerable period of time.

At this juncture we must make an important point: AIDS itself does not kill anyone. The disease affects the body's ability to fend off a number of diseases that the normal immune system copes with on a daily basis. Disability, pain, and death usually result from these opportunistic infections that then ravage the undefended individual. For example, one of the most common opportunistic infections, pneumocystis carinii pneumonia comes from a protozoa that most of us carry in our bodies. Our immune systems simply keep it at bay. The same is true of some CMV infections that attack PWAs. On the other hand, PWAs may also be especially vulnerable to diseases from outside of their own bodies.

The "Hierarchy" of Categories

Within the gay male world there is a distinction or a hierarchy that has grown up around the phases or categories that we have just discussed. At the top of the heap is the person who has tested HIV−, the person who has not been exposed to the virus. Generally, these are considered to be the "lucky ones." They may also be considered the "good ones," the ones who did not involve themselves with multiple sex partners or in less virtuous forms of sexual activity. In actual fact, this may not be true, but the perception remains.

Next come those whose status is unclear; they have not been tested and do not want to know their HIV status for various reasons. They can still avoid dealing directly with others around HIV. They do not have to risk compromising their desirability. For some, though, the burden of knowing that they are positive might produce more anxiety than they feel prepared to handle.

Next come those who are HIV +, who still generally do not see themselves as sick. In fact, many HIV + men still insist that as long as they have "safer sex" they do not need to inform their sex partners of their HIV status. Some HIV + men take active steps to maintain their health. Some go into deep denial, insisting that if they get sick they will take the necessary steps. Some get very depressed or quite psychosomatic. The range of reactions varies, but some level of anxiety infects most.

The PWARC has some clear evidence that he is sick, but he still doesn't have "it." There is an interesting level of denial that may develop in the ARC phase that parallels the artificial medical distinction between ARC and AIDS. The truth is that no real distinction exists, except in people's minds. I have seen PWARCs with virtually no remaining T-helper cells. No one can really explain what keeps them alive and relatively well. Then I have seen PWAs with T-helper cell counts of 300–400, and they, too, may appear quite healthy. The PWA in this situation may actually be healthier than the PWARC, yet the PWA carries the more serious diagnosis. (A young man I saw in therapy who had just survived the treatment for HIV-related lymphoma and whose T-helper cell count was 50 adamantly insisted that he did not have AIDS; technically, he was correct. This kind of denial often leads to rather severe depression when someone like this young man develops an infection that does change his diagnosis.)

The PWA falls on the bottom of the diagnostic totem pole,

even though, as we just pointed out, he may be healthier than his ARC compatriot. I make this point because this is a distinction that your clients may make. If you tell most PWARCs that in reality they have AIDS, they will reject that premise because the diagnosis of AIDS may require a significant shift in thinking.

Standard Treatments

Some of the clients you see may be on standard regimens such as the anti-viral AZT or the pneumocystis-preventing aerosolized pentamadine. You would do well to familiarize yourself with some of these treatments, bearing in mind that many AIDS drug treatments are "for life" — it is not simply a question of taking a drug for ten days or so and then recovering. For many AIDS patients, if the drug stops, the infection recurs, which gives life a totally different perspective. The ingestion of pills every day and night reminds you that you are sick and that recovery in terms of cure is still not available. It also reinforces your terrible vulnerability.

Unconventional Treatments

As with many potentially terminal diseases, a plethora of physical and emotional treatments have emerged for dealing with AIDS. We will not review them here. Just be aware that sometimes clients are very secretive about what they are taking or whom they are seeing. PWAs may see a variety of practitioners without informing the various practitioners. This includes psychotherapists. Do not assume that your client sees only you (other sources of support may prove beneficial, as we will discuss later in this chapter, but seeing multiple therapists generally causes confusion).

AIDS Dementia

As a psychologist I am often asked, "How can you distinguish between depression and AIDS dementia?" I wish I had a good answer. Obviously, many PWAs exhibit signs of depression, including loss of motivation, ennui, and forget-fulness. More and more the medical folks are demonstrating that a large percentage of HIV+ patients shows evidence of neurological involvement, ranging from loss of motor skills to Alzheimer-like dementias. Gross dementia is easily recog-nizable, but subtle signs evade detection. What is attribut-able to depression and anxiety and what to neurological in-volvement? At the present time, there is no readily available, inexpensive and useful way to make these distinctions. We can predict, however, that as treatments improve for the various opportunistic infections, we will see more AIDS de-mentia, simply because people will survive for a longer peri-od of time.

Issues of Control

Probably never before in history has there been a body of patients so well-informed and so determined to have their say in the treatment of an illness. Many gay PWAs are high-ly educated, successful, and assertive males. Many know as much or more than their physicians about the illness, and they are not bound by medical convention in terms of look-ing at possible interventions – physical, spiritual, and emo-tional. Many (not all) are determined to take charge of their treatments or, at least, to participate in treatment as equal partners. These PWAs do not acquiesce to the orders of their physicians, nor do they necessarily buy the interventions of their therapists.

One client came to me at the insistence of his physician. The physician told me that this PWA was driving his office staff crazy with his demands and his questions concerning what was being done. Some of the physician's concerns were justified. The PWA was a demanding individual, who sometimes wanted answers where there were none. Still, I was hard-pressed to tell the client to act in a more compliant fashion, when my experience with cancer patients had taught me that the more compliant patients recovered less often and died sooner!

Not all PWAs fit this description, however. At the other

extreme, you will find PWAs who just want someone to take care of them. This is probably true in any patient population, but especially in a group where people feel cutoff and alienated from a large segment of society.

Among the more assertive members of this population, loss of control is a major fear. Many men express the opinion that they do not fear death, but they do fear the debilitating process associated with the progression of the disease. And as males, they do not find it easy to ask for help, from partners, who are also males, from families, from whom they may have become estranged, or from a world this has always appeared more than a little judgmental. They will fight to stay in charge, which may prove to be their greatest asset.

Gay Self-image

Many gay men retain a lingering negative self-image, not surprising after years of negative reinforcement. The self-image issue comes out in several ways. First, on some level, there are those who want to die – because they feel bad about what they are, and because they fear becoming "tired, old queens," lonely and unattractive. This self-image issue is, more often than not, a covert one. Second, they are often more concerned about protecting their families from unpleasant information than they are about their own survival. More on the family follows.

THE GAY PWA FAMILY OF ORIGIN

Cutoffs and Stigma

The turmoil created by the AIDS diagnosis in the PWA family of origin has received little attention from those working with this disease. Partly this is because of geographical distance that often exits between son and family; partly it is because families turn inward as a result of this disease, cutting off from other family members, friends, neighbors, church and business associates. Shame and stigma still surround this disease, and families may go to great measures to

protect themselves and to maintain their secret. Recently I
heard of a family who, upon the death of their son, offered
the physician money to keep AIDS off of the death certifi-
cate!

Double Death Syndrome

Few families have been kept abreast of the progression of
this disease by those affected, their sons. In fact, a great
many PWA families have had no explicit understanding of
their sons' sexual orientation prior to diagnosis. In these
cases, families may experience what I have called the "double death syndrome" – a call from the hospital informs them
that their son has AIDS and soon they discover that their
son is gay. Because of the publicity that now surrounds the
disease, fewer families experience this double jolt today, but
some still do and will in the future. It is embedded in the
fabric of the cutoff process.

Parental Blame

Most parents blame themselves. Sometimes they blame
each other. Usually mothers shoulder more guilt, since the
responsibility for the proper raising of the children falls on
her. After initial anger, disbelief, or even acceptance, they
ask themselves. "Where did I go wrong?" First they blame
themselves for having failed in the process of parenting.
Then they blame themselves for their son's illness. During
some undefined initial period, it doesn't matter how much
material you offer parents on the origins of homosexuality.
Most of them will still believe that they have done something wrong to cause it. Some parents never give up the guilt
and the self-examination process that goes with their son's
homosexuality. It seems to be part of an almost universal
homophobia.

Recently a mother of a PWA sat with her son in my office.
She was the mother of three sons, two of whom were gay and
HIV+. We touched on the strain of having one son sick and
the other a potential candidate for the disease. She avoided

any real discussion of this issue. I switched to my standard rap about what we know about the causes of homosexuality, that our best guesses involve a major biological component, that hundreds of genograms from men in my practice give no indication of recurrent family patterns or areas where parents have "gone wrong." She sat there impassively, taking it all in. When I finished, I said to her, "Now you don't believe any of this, do you?" She shook her head in the negative.

Protecting Parents

Many gay men go to great lengths to protect their parents from the truth about their sexuality. They may fear parental rejection, but they also may be keenly aware of how much blame the parents will assume. Several years ago I was called on to see a patient in the hospital. His physician told me that he needed to be seen within the next 24 hours, for she thought that he would probably be on a respirator after that. His parents, fundamentalist Christians, did not know that he was gay or that he had AIDS, and they were driving to Atlanta that day. When I went to the hospital, I found an extremely weak 28-year-old man, who was more concerned about how his parents would react than he was about his own survival.

We worked for several hours on how he would tell his parents. They arrived in the middle of the night, and he told them. Initially they reacted much better than what he had expected (they developed a very intransigent attitude some weeks later). Twenty-four hours later he began what was termed a miraculous turnaround. One week later he left the hospital under his own power. Clearly, the energy he had used to protect his parents and to worry about their reaction was mobilized to help effect his recovery.

Other Family Members

No one can ever make general statements about how brothers, sisters, grandparents, aunts, uncles, etc., will react in a crisis. Obviously, every family is different, and reactions vary widely. Sometimes grandparents, having seen more of life and being generally removed from a direct line of responsibility, will prove to be strong allies. Sometimes not. At least some grandparents can identify with the loss of peers. Sometimes siblings rally around their brother. Sometimes they close doors in order to protect their own children from exposure, no matter how impossible exposure might be. Sometimes siblings will push to protect parents. Sometimes parents want to shield siblings.

One thing that the therapist can expect in most situations: The family will move to a more isolated, cutoff position in regard to this disease. Sincere offers of support notwithstanding, the family members will withdraw from the traditional supports upon which they would rely in other crisis situations. Compounding this isolation is the lack of interaction with the PWA's social network.

Caretaking and Community

Some PWAs go home to die. Loss of job, inadequate insurance, physical infirmity, minimal caretaking resources – all may lead the PWA back home. Sometimes it is simply love and caring, but few adult males willingly choose parental care in the setting of their childhood community. Once again we encounter the stigma of the disease. Sometimes the family may have no choice, as often happens with the elderly. But for the elderly there is sympathy and some support from outside the family. Realistically or not, most families fear the reactions of their neighbors to this disease.

The PWA who returns home usually does so with no community support or network of his own. He may have previously eschewed the connections with his past in order to protect himself and his family. He may return home out of necessity to an environment that disapproves of him, his lifestyle, and his disease. He may return home, leaving a lover behind, because economic and medical circumstances dictate it.

Some PWAs in major cities prefer the care they can get

from friends or from community resources that have been established to provide care. Sometimes this process excludes family members, who feel more pained because they carry guilt about their "defective" childrearing. Clearly, the need exists for more networking of families, friends, and institutions. We will look at an innovative approach to this problem later in this chapter.

Isolation and Bereavement

PWAs die. Families and friends go their separate ways. Sometimes the family takes the body home for a private funeral, despite the last wishes of the deceased (in Georgia your next-of-kin owns your body after your death). Friends may be left without any ritual to mark the passage. Families often substitute more acceptable causes of death in quick, private funerals. Since they fear discovery, they often mourn in isolation, from the community and from each other.

PWAS AND PARTNERS

Dealing with PWAs who are coupled adds a different dimension and an additional resource to the process. It also has the potential for additional complications. We must begin with the obvious: Relationships plagued by underlying difficulties before the illness will continue to exhibit those underlying difficulties after diagnosis. Except in some cases, the difficulties become unspoken—they go underground in the name of protection.

The PWA and his partner may function under a number of different conditions: (1) Both may have AIDS and both may have been affected by debilitating conditions; (2) one may have AIDS, the other ARC, and both may function with varying degrees of wellness/illness; (3) one may have AIDS and the other may be only HIV+; (4) one may have AIDS and the other may be HIV−.

The last situation—where one person in a couple has AIDS and the other is HIV − −surprises many people; yet, it really is not that unusual. I have seen a number of couples in this situation, even when they have both been together over a long period of time and have remained sexually active. Most likely the form of their sexual involvement contributes a good deal to a partner's remaining HIV −.

Luckily, I have seen or heard of few couples in the first situation, especially where both are in debilitated states simultaneously. Recently, however, I have seen many more instances like this. When both experience acute difficulties at the same time, usually friends, paid staff, or family members must be called on to provide care or one or both must return home to the family of origin. Sometimes two single PWAs will meet and couple during the course of the illness, in which case any counseling must deal with the issue of future illness, both emotionally and in terms of caretaking arrangements. Many men will push to avoid any discussion of illness and caretaking on the grounds that the consideration of such issues is negative and they wish to remain positive in their outlook. Obviously such things as wills, living wills, power of attorney, and caretaking can best be handled while people are healthy and not in a crisis state. The therapist may frame the consideration of such future arrangements as a way of getting them out of the way and thus freeing up energy for *living*.

The Coupling/Uncoupling Dilemma

Several potential dilemmas exist for couples dealing with this disease. The first is peculiar to HIV, while the second exists with other potentially terminal or potentially chronic illnesses.

Concerning HIV specifically, the diagnosis of an HIV + condition in one or both partners may evoke several reactions. They may pull closer together and, in fact, look quite enmeshed. They may decide to uncouple and to experience a greater variety of sexual partners or to find the ideal romance while they are still well (a "grass is greener" phenomenon). They may split, ostensibly to protect the HIV − partner.

Concerning couples in general, the specter of potentially terminal or chronic illness throws the undiagnosed partner into a quandary, especially if the relationship has had weak spots to begin with. If he leaves, he experiences guilt and the world may label him as an unfeeling jerk. If he stays, he must shoulder the burden of caretaking and will certainly experience the feelings of being trapped. This is true for AIDS, for cancer, for head injuries, etc. Where there is potentially terminal or serious chronic illness, we will see this dilemma. The hardest part of that no "correct" choice exists. The healthy partner remains "between a rock and a hard place."

What remains different for gay male couples is gender. As we have already seen, men do not perform caretaking tasks in our culture as easily as do women. Also, family members may take over certain caretaking tasks that a partner wishes to perform; since they may not really recognize the relationship, and since they may perceive that they can do things better than another man could, the PWA's partner may get squeezed out. Sometimes it is a relief. Sometimes it generates anger and isolation. Sometimes both. The art of dealing effectively with this crisis involves creating an atmosphere where people feel useful without feeling overburdened—not an easy accomplishment. Often, because of cutoffs, the burden of physical and emotional caretaking falls, on a very few people. If the burden falls primarily on the PWA's partner, it may prove too much for him to handle.

Cutoffs, Again

Gerry and Joseph appeared in my office for what they described as another round of communication problems. They had been together for ten years, and I had seen them six years before for basically the same complaint. At that time, we had made real progress, and they had continued to build a satisfying and productive relationship that had amazed family and friends. This visit, though, something did not ring true. After about 50 minutes of exploring their

identified problem, I asked, "Well, what's your HIV status?"
Silence. "Hey guys," I repeated, "what's your HIV status?"
Finally, after more hesitation, Gerry replied that he had been
diagnosed with ARC, and that he had been on AZT for several months.

These two men, whom I knew reasonably well, had not
planned to reveal this information to me. In fact, Joseph,
who was HIV−, had insisted that Gerry not tell *anyone*
about his diagnosis. Gerry had agreed. As a result, these two
men were feeling tremendous pressure on their relationship.
Gerry had no one but Joseph with whom to discuss his fears,
and Joseph was not too receptive to those discussions anyway. Joseph had no one with whom to discuss his anxieties
about Gerry and about the future.

What was Joseph's reluctance all about? Well, first there
was the ubiquitous denial. Denial characterizes so much of
the interactions around AIDS. The world and the medical
establishment practiced denial for years. The heterosexual
community is still in some forms of denial. And young gay
men, who have practiced their persuasion like a semi-private
cult for years, do not have the emotional resources to open
themselves up for additional judgment from either the
straight world or the gay world. A good deal of the mystique
of the gay male world rests on youth, health, and good looks.
Anything that jeopardizes the mystique requires immediate
corrective action. Usually corrective action involves work-
outs, hair dye, a new wardrobe, or a diet. In the case of
AIDS, very few options exist. In other words, gay men
thought that if they lived their lives in a prescribed, private
way, they could avoid a good many confrontations concerning their lifestyle, that they had a certain number of good
years to do what they wanted sexually and socially. AIDS
blew apart the closet.

So a great many gay men use denial as a defense. (And a
certain amount of denial is necessary just to keep one's sani-
ty in the face of a potentially terminal illness.) They continue
to practice unsafe sex as if the risk of HIV infection really
does not exist. They deny that an HIV+ status really means

that there is a potential danger, and they avoid investigating the steps that might prolong their good health. They deny that severe ARC rarely differs from a diagnosis of AIDS.

They deny, too, to avoid being stigmatized in their own community. The AIDS diagnosis limits the amount of sexual freedom that one can exercise, especially if the effects of the disease are physically obvious. For gay men, the freedom to exercise their sexuality represents one of the few real freedoms they have had. Not all men have chosen to exercise this freedom, but the option has remained as a possibility. AIDS limits that freedom, closes the door on that possibility. In fact, it may close the door on sexual relationships, period.

We have already discussed the issue of gay self-image. Many gay men continue to harbor deep feelings about the sin of their sexuality. The diagnosis of AIDS confirms to many that they have done something wrong. Many gay men believe that this *is* a gay disease, despite evidence to the contrary. This is an *emotional* issue. A great many men have "come out" have chosen to celebrate their sexuality after years of repression and suppression. They naturally have a difficult time accepting that any unbridled celebration has ended.

For Gerry and Joseph the diagnosis involved a number of issues on many levels. On a superficial level, it threatened their sexual style. For most of their ten years together, they had relied on "three ways"—involving a third party in their mutual sexual relationship. The news that Gerry had ARC meant that they either would have to forego their arrangements or not be honest with a third person about possible dangers. Foregoing their sexual arrangement meant yet another cutoff, albeit of a superficial nature. The change meant an unbalancing of their relationship in a way that had helped it to work throughout most of their history.

For gay male couples in general, who have forged a certain amount of security in an insecure environment, the AIDS diagnosis represents a threat on a very deep level. Coupling with another man may mean security, protection, insulation from the assaults of a hostile, heterosexual world. In a stable coupled relationship the partners can enjoy some of the illusion that they are just like everyone else – comfortable, married people. AIDS threatens that idea to the very core. Suddenly there is the specter of disability, death, loneliness, lack of support, and fears for the remaining partner's own health. Recovery and support remain more difficult in a world of cutoffs.

Gerry and Joseph's reaction to Gerry's diagnosis is quite typical; yet, this reaction moves this couple in distress in the *wrong* direction. This kind of cutoff has been seen in at least one other population. My colleague Michael Berger noted a number of years ago that families with severely handicapped children cut themselves off from their networks. In the process, typically the mother became an expert on the disability and threw herself into the process of dealing with it, mostly alone. Fathers involved themselves more thoroughly in work, ostensibly to earn the money that might be needed for the care of the child. Family, friends, neighbors and business associates got closed out of any process and usually any meaningful interaction with the family. The children in these scenarios always did worse than children in families where the networks were opened up, generally with the help of professional intervention.

Gay males with AIDS react in a similar fashion, except for them the cutoffs have always been present. The idea that opening up their networks may improve their prognosis is the basis of an idea that will be discussed later in this chapter. When working to expand networks, the therapist must remain familiar with all aspects of illness, cutoffs, social reactions, and the sanctity of the couple. For example, in a situation where the undiagnosed lover has taken on the lion's share of the responsibility in the area of caretaking and support, that individual may become overburdened by the sheer demands of the situation. In addition, he may not have an adequate support system of his own in the circumstances. Spreading the burden may be desirable from a therapeutic standpoint, but the intervention must take into account the feelings of the caretaker in losing *too much* responsibility and not feeling useful. If family members are called in, will they take over, while cutting the lover completely out of the job he has struggled to maintain? If friends provide more support for the caregiver, will he begin to feel too much like a patient?

Death, Dying and Other Issues

Since we are dealing with an illness of a highly terminal nature, we must, of course, observe the Kübler-Ross progression of denial, anger, bargaining, depression, and acceptance (not necessarily in that order). We have already discussed how denial becomes a hallmark issue. Because this population is so young, bargaining is also very evident, but maybe no more so than with other illnesses. Many PWAs spend their time bargaining for more without using whatever time they have to pursue some goal or interest. Of course, you need to be aware that many gay men pursue their sexual interests with a high degree of energy; this pursuit often leaves very little time for the formulation of other goals and interests in their lives. The young or even middle-aged gay man who has come out may live for his sexuality to the exclusion of many other things. (In fact, many gay men come into therapy as they enter their thirties because they realize in one way or another that they have given very little thought to what they want to do with their lives, aside from being gay.)

Acceptance of death also represents a difficult issue for so young a population. Those who have experienced more of life are obviously in a better position to put their lives in perspective. The client with a partner may be in a better position to gain this perspective, since coupled gay men typically have made more plans and set more goals than men who have continued to have multiple partners.

Some other more concrete issues remain for the couple: (1) the blaming of the PWA's partner by the family-of-origin; (2) the status of the lover as a family member at home, hospital, funeral, and after death; and (3) attention focused on the PWA to the exclusion of his partner. These concerns and others need to be addressed in the therapy process or through other interventions.

INTERVENTIONS

Standard psychotherapy modes may prove helpful to couples dealing with AIDS, but they will probably also prove inadequate. The needs that these couples experience often go beyond what can occur in the therapist's office. It should already be evident that some family work and community networking may play a significant part in helping the couple deal with AIDS. In fact, some couples with networks in place and families standing by, who have dealt with cutoffs before diagnosis or in early stages of the disease, may do quite well without standard psychotherapy interventions. All couples affected by this disease do best with some form of outside support in place.

The amount and the effectiveness of community resources depend to a large extent on where people live. Naturally, large metropolitan areas with large gay populations tend to offer more resources. Resources in major cities may include such things as HIV+ support groups, PWA support groups, PWA partner support groups, family support groups, couple support groups, community dinners for PWAs, daily meals for PWAs, group housing, hospice-type care, legal counseling, referral services, network enhancement programs, etc.

Support Groups

Various support groups may prove invaluable to the PWA and his partner in dealing with the disease. On the positive side, these groups often link people who otherwise would not know about each other. Friendships, partnerships, and good supports often result. However, there are some inherent problems with some of the group resources. As a therapist you need to be aware of these problems or limitations, since a great many of the PWA couples you will see have probably already had some experience with support groups before coming to see you.

First, most support group networks are not systemic, so they tend to deal with problems in a very linear fashion. For example, they may consistently separate partners into PWA groups and partner groups or PWA groups and family groups. This usually happens because social service providers as a rule do not think systemically and case management logistics make such homogeneous groupings more manageable.

Second, many of the PWA-related support groups are run by agencies or social service networks set up to deal with AIDS. Many do a creditable job. Many are "drop-in" groups with no set membership run by group facilitators who have very little training. The drop-in nature of any group limits its effectiveness in terms of progressive support. Whenever the composition changes significantly, the group recycles back to the beginning, so that regular attendees may never have the opportunity to get past a certain point. Many times the facilitators or organizers are completely unaware of this issue.

Third, untrained facilitators allow the group to move in unproductive or even destructive directions. Many PWAs complain that their support groups turn into sessions concerning who has the worst horror story to tell this week. Other times the group supports massive denial that may contribute to dysfunction.

Fourth, the public nature of the support group attracts a socioeconomically heterogeneous population. Many middle and upper-middle class PWAs reject this mixture, feeling that they have nothing in common with others in the group (who may include IV drug abusers). It is unfortunate that this kind of prejudice exists, but it does, and you may as well be prepared to deal with it. You will often find it difficult to persuade your private therapy clients to attend groups open to the public, especially if they have previously had a bad experience with such a group. Private practice support groups often feel more comfortable for such clients, but they cost money, can be difficult to organize, and exclude those who are not in a position to pay.

Fifth, many PWA are concerned that public airing of their health situation will result in violation of their confidentiality. They do not trust that word will not get around. Often they are correct. Health providers or those in health-related careers such as psychotherapists may find that their participation in a support group as a member results in a diminished practice.

Despite these limitations, I continue to encourage clients and friends to attend some sort of support group or perhaps to start one of their own. Like Alcoholics Anonymous, different groups work for different people. If resources permit and a group does not suit you, then visit another group, but don't just give up. Once again, the right group with the right facilitator may help to provide a lot of what a PWA and his partner require.

Couples Therapy

A PWA and his therapist may be tempted to embark on individual therapy sessions. I do not recommend it any more than I would recommend handling marital problems in individual therapy. The partner needs to contribute to the process, to be aware of issues paramount to both of them. And individual therapy encourages the very cutoff process we need to avoid.

Gay male couples will seek your help at various stages of the illness, ranging from an initial HIV+ test result to the final stages of dying. Where you start is determined by what they have already dealt with, what they know, and how much time you will have with them.

The person who tests HIV+ will probably come to see you in somewhat of a crisis situation, perhaps immediately after test results, but more likely after it has all had a chance to sink in. The visit may be triggered by a friend who has recently received an AIDS diagnosis or someone taking a turn for the worse or simply by the realization that one's immortality is threatened. Generally, people who are just HIV+ do not drop in just for a chat; there is usually some panic that has propelled them to your office. Usually they will come alone. It is the kind of situation where the HIV+ person has talked to his partner and together they have done some processing. When anxiety continues to build, the partner may say, "You need to see someone!" At this stage I encourage the client to bring his partner in with him. The tendency to shrink one's network may begin at just this point. Also, dealing with this crisis individually may encourage secrets or prevent the kind of sharing that needs to take place between the partners. A couple session is a good time to check out the resources that the partner brings to the situation. He may need help in getting his supports in place.

At the point of initial identification of the virus presence, the couple often needs information on what this all means. If the partners do not have basic information about the disease, this is the time for them to get it. You might also check to see whether the person has a regular physician on whom he can rely to follow his progress. A physician who has had experience with PWAs is definitely preferred. If you do not feel competent to handle this educational process, then you need to refer the couple to a source that handles this kind of work.

You can safely bet that someone who is HIV+ and whose T4 cells remain reasonably high will sink back into comfortable denial once this initial anxiety has passed. Of course, there are some who will obsess about their status, but on the whole a comfortable denial takes over. Once the partners have the information they need to have about safe sex, regular check-ins with the physician, advice on supports, a mechanism for talking to each other, there is really no need to press hard on this denial. In fact, at this stage they probably won't be interested in anything more than a few sessions to diffuse the crisis. Then they may go back to living as normally as possible, which may prove to be very normally. A little denial can be a good thing.

Still, at this stage you may begin to deal with issues of telling family (usually avoided at this point), friends, partner's family, work associates. Generally, if the person is healthy, there may be few compelling reasons to deal with business associates, partner's family, and some friends. The couple should be encouraged, though, to share the situation with *someone*, be it family, friends, or a good support group for HIV+ people. Sharing with someone at this stage reduces the likelihood that they will limit their network as they go along; it also takes some of the pressure off their relationship. Sometimes you will find that the partners retreat into denial without taking your suggestions about expanding their network seriously. Yet, quite often down the road they will begin to implement these suggestions; they will come back to see you a year later and tell you that just last month or last summer they told Aunt Susie and Uncle Herbert and now they are in regular contact.

Many young client couples, in their twenties or even thirties, have a difficult time dealing with their vulnerability. A good support group may help them to process this issue over a period of time. They can see others who are managing, obtain some perspective from older group members, and begin to deal with the reality that some things just won't go away. A good support group may also provide resources for them to investigate in order to stay as healthy as possible. One of the most frustrating things to deal with at this point in the disease is the doing-nothing-and-waiting part. Investigating resources provides a measure of feeling in control.

You might also encourage couples to develop some joint goals, if they do not already have them, preferably short- to medium-term goals (where results come sooner, so there is less waiting piled on waiting). Be careful that you do not present this idea as a gloom and doom proposition. Having joint, obtainable goals—perhaps even speeding up goals they had discussed for the future—will help couples feel as if they are living, not just waiting, and hold the prospect for more mutual support.

One of the most difficult parts of working with HIV disease is maintaining reasonable optimism along with reasonable reality. You must not diffuse reasonable hope, nor should you encourage foolish optimism that leads to denial (and sometimes to an avoidance of reasonable medical interventions). Do not be afraid to talk openly about realistic prospects, but do not take a you-will-die-soon stance. Recent research shows that those who maintain good attitudes and who progress toward goals live longer with this disease then those who give up.

Once again, you can expect that those couples who begin with you at this point in the disease will check back from time to time for reassurance and support. You may again begin to function as part of the expanded network; however, in my view the natural support network holds the most potential for those dealing with AIDS. Someone who is paid to care, if you will, can never take the place of good, natural supports and real intimacy. Certainly, the therapist can help a person or a couple to process issues that might prove burdensome or awkward for family and friends to deal with. However, too much dependence on therapy in this situation can actually promote the shrinking of the network, to the clients' disadvantage in the long run.

The most difficult place to begin couple therapy is in the general hospital, with a PWA in medical crisis. Emotionally, you cannot deny the suggestion of death. Logistically, you must deal with medical people, friends, and hospital personnel who come in and out of the room or ward and who do not recognize you in your professional capacity. If you are to get any work done in this setting, it helps to have the cooperation of the admitting physician and to inform the nursing staff about your function. Many times you will find the nursing staff to be highly cooperative. If they regularly deal with AIDS patients, they are sometimes relieved to meet someone who will share the burden of providing support. Many nurses get quite attached the their PWA patients (a number of male nurses are gay males), and sometimes they will take on too much of the emotional burden. At any rate, tell them why you are there and request a DO NOT DISTURB situation if you need one.

Some hospitals permit family members and partners to sleep overnight in a patient's room. This may be the first real contact that family and partner have had. Who stays in the room may be the subject of some disagreement. If family members have just recently been notified about the illness, they may ask you for information and help, but often they do not. If a partner is present with family, and if friends also visit, you have an opportunity to do some networking. Take it – the opportunity may not open up again any time soon.

If a PWA is truly on his deathbed and you already have a relationship with the couple, you can help them deal with approaching death. If the PWA is ill but not dying, you can help the couple by focusing on the kinds of things they might set as goals *after* the PWA's release. In cases of severe illness and surgery, you can enhance the person's chances of survival and even diminish the duration of a hospital stay by planning ahead with post-recovery goals.

Unless you work in a hospital setting, most of your work with PWA couples will take place on an ongoing basis, usually after one or both have received an AIDS or an ARC diagnosis and have required some form of major medical intervention, such as transfusions or ongoing medication. Often it takes the advent of infection, medication side-effects, or the scare of chronic weight loss to bring home the reality of the disease.

As we have already emphasized, serious preexisting relationship issues aside, the major overall emphasis with PWA couples should be on the network. Support for the couple, the individuals, the family, the friends, and business associates is usually most effective when it comes from the resources available to them in the community. This may seem like a strange thing for a therapist to say, but it is true. Therapeutic interventions that help to pull together networks provide the best support for these couples.

Couples therapy can help to elucidate and process many of the tensions and anxieties that will develop between the partners. It can help to circumvent unproductive sequences that develop as a result of the illness. It can work on the evolution of death and dying issues. Still, the most productive focus throughout therapy will be on making sure that as many supports as possible come together for all the people involved.

On a very concrete level, you need to begin with issues of wills and arrangements for caretaking, finances, living wills. etc. The importance of having these things in order so that the couple can concentrate on living cannot be overstated.

Donald came to see me in a somewhat agitated state. He and Lincoln had been together for 14 years, in a monogamous relationship. Three months before, without previous warning, Lincoln, 45, developed a case of *pneumocystis* and was hospitalized. (Either Lincoln had violated their agreement about monogamy, which Donald seriously doubted, or he had been exposed to the virus in the mid-1970s!). He spent about six week in the hospital and then several weeks at home recovering. He had recently returned to work in a full-time capacity. Donald reported that his partner had lost weight, was constantly tired, and that the pressures of his job were taking their toll. Donald had provided all the major caretaking for Lincoln, sleeping at the hospital in the early weeks, visiting thereafter, waiting on him after his return home.

During all this the two men had done little talking about the stresses of the illness on each other or anything about the future. Donald had talked with his aunt, who knew them as a couple, but otherwise he had kept to himself. Donald was physically and emotionally spent.

After the initial session with Donald alone, I encouraged him to check with Lincoln so that we could make an appointment for the two of them. Since they owned a home, several automobiles, and some additional property together, I asked whether they had seen an attorney about legal arrangements, power of attorney in the event in Lincoln's incapacity, etc. Donald replied that they had talked about doing all of those things for years, but had neglected to do anything about them. And, he continued, in the midst of all the illness he hadn't wanted to bring any of this up with Lincoln. He said that Lincoln's relatives were reasonable people who knew that they were a couple and that he had no concerns about any trouble they might make in the case of Lincoln's death.

Because of some business travel, they were unable to schedule an appointment for several weeks. The weekend before their visit Donald called me at home to tell me that he had come home on Friday evening to find Lincoln dead on the bedroom floor. The cause of death was a heart attack. We scheduled several appointments in the following weeks to help him deal with his grieving. During that time, their being no will, he sat down with his attorney. Lincoln's family also saw an attorney. There was no question that Donald would get Lincoln's life insurance, since he was the beneficiary, but Lincoln's family planned to go to court to get the men's home, cars and property, all of which were in Lincoln's name!

So do not skirt the issue of arrangements in early sessions. Actually, one of the challenges of working with PWA couples is to avoiding skirting things in general. With practice you will learn to be direct and honest without being threatening. Without directness, denial will flourish.

Even when one partner has AIDS, the therapist must not focus on the identified patient. Both men will have issues about dying, whether they are about leaving or about being left. Both men will have issues about living, whether it's business as usual or stepping up the timetable. Both men may be tentative about what they ask of each other, as well as what they ask of others outside the relationship.

Arnold and Allen had spent the last six years together. They had met shortly after college and had lived together ever since. Both came from the same city, but they had not known each other growing up. Both were climbing the career ladder in different businesses. Arnold came to see me by himself. He had planned a trip home several weeks hence, and he planned to tell his family about his ARC diagnosis at that time. He wanted help in deciding how to approach them. We spent a long session working out the best combinations of people to deal with (I use a genogram to help me understand family patterns and relationships).

After his return I had him schedule an appointment that would include Allen, too. Both men were HIV+. Arnold's T4 cell count had started up at 150 at the time of testing, and it had dropped to a low of 25 just before he came to see me. Allen's T4 counts began at 225 and they had climbed to 550 in recent months. Both men had begun AZT some months before, and otherwise had followed the same regimens. Allen tolerated AZT very well and had benefited from it. Arnold had tolerated it badly and required numerous transfusions. Allen did not talk to Arnold much about what was going on. Although he had remained very supportive, he felt very guilty that he had done so well on the same treatment that seemed to be making Arnold worse. The two of them had initially told several couple friends about their diagnoses, but basically neither one had developed friends with whom they could really share their feelings and anxieties. They both felt inclined to protect each other from too much explicit talk about what was going on.

Breaking into the protective stance that the partners may take toward each other, as well as toward family members and friends, becomes an important focus of therapy. You also need to tune into protective stances outside the couple relationship, with family members and friends acting in all good faith to protect the PWA, often creating triangles and encouraging secrets in their pursuit of what they see as helpfulness.

In this case, since Arnold had taken steps to tell family members (they had responded in a very positive way), he had paved the way for the two of them to begin building on and linking their support networks.

Enhancing Networks

Several times I have alluded to a somewhat innovative approach to AIDS support and counseling. It falls under the rubric of network enhancement. Thanks to a generous grant from the Robert Wood Johnson Foundation, we have recently begun to implement this approach.

I mentioned earlier that Dr. Michael Berger and I had learned that families with handicapped children tended to cutoff from their support networks shortly after learning about their child's handicap. In addition, the work of another colleague at the Atlanta Institute for Family Studies, Dr. Carrell Dammann, had indicated that network meetings often led to an improved environment for cancer patients. So we began to think about more networking with PWAs. I knew that there was a problem implicit in this approach. PWAs often have two very separate networks – a friend network and a family network, often *very* separate. So I began to think about incorporating some of the Link Therapy that I had heard Dr. Judith Landau-Stanton discuss a few years earlier.

Dr. Landau-Stanton, originally from South Africa, had worked with families where the grandparents were literally just out of the bush, and the grandchildren were street-wise city kids. The parents were often caught in a value squeeze, which perpetuated the presenting problems. Dr. Landau-Stanton developed a therapy scheme that involved selecting what she called a "link therapist" from somewhere in the extended family. This link therapist had the ability to talk to all the elements in the family, to bridge the value gap. She then worked with the link therapist and had the link therapist make the interventions in the family.

In a somewhat similar way, gay men often develop separate networks with very different values. Often no one really functions as a bridge between these separate networks. In times of health such linkage often seemed unimportant. In times of illness, however, the value of linking these networks becomes crystal clear. The PWA needs maximum support. Partners and friends need support, and families need support. The network split and the existing cutoffs may preclude anyone's getting the needed support.

The current three-year project (Project Prevail) explores the use of a networking approach enhanced by the use of a link therapist or therapists selected from the PWA's natural support network.

CONCLUSION

Skillful, useful couples therapy provides a challenge for all family systems therapists. A potentially terminal illness adds another dimension; when that illness is AIDS the issues are more complex still.

The therapist must begin with some understanding of how gay male couples operate apart from this illness. Then he or she must become somewhat conversant with the different aspects of this disease. And finally, the situation calls for the additional resources necessary to delve into networking strategies.

Therapist burnout is a very real issue in working with PWAs. If you work with a large number of PWAs, there spouses and families, I strongly recommend some sort of support for *you!* That is yet another reason for developing natural supports for these couples. Every report indicates that the number of PWAs will increase dramatically in the next five years. The professional community will never be able to handle the needs of PWAs and their partners relaying on traditional approaches. What is more, the needs of surviving families and friends, largely ignored at the present time, require better linkages in the community. Sheer numbers will dictate a more efficient approach.

9

ALCOHOL, DRUGS, AND ADDITIONAL THERAPY CONCERNS

To this point I have said little about the effects of alcohol, drugs, and related problems on the gay and lesbian couple – this despite the fact that prevailing thought has it that gay men and lesbians experience more alcohol and drug problems than the population in general. I do not dispute this observation, and, of course, I see my share of alcohol and drug problems in gay and straight clients alike. It is no surprise that a population that has historically been very bar-oriented and that experiences more than the normal struggle with self-image would turn to mood-altering substances as a partial solution to life's problems.

Nor am I surprised to find a good bit of domestic violence among such couples, especially since domestic violence is closely linked to alcohol and drug abuse. I must confess that I have seen far less domestic violence than many other therapists, probably because I do not enjoy working with violent situations. Still this book would be incomplete without at least passing commentary on these problems.

ALCOHOL AND DRUGS

Like most of my colleagues, I refer many clients with alcohol and drug problems to Alcoholics Anonymous, Narcotics Anonymous and related organizations as ancillary treatment. (In this chapter I will use AA as a generic label for all the related 12-step programs.) I do it, but that does not mean that I necessarily like it. Allow me to elaborate. AA and its 12-step philosophy work for some people. At the moment AA is probably the single best thing we have for dealing with substance abuse problems. The same goes for Alanon, although I actually feel that Alanon helps more people strictly in its support function. Too many people who live with the ravages of substance abuse deny themselves the support they need to cope with drinking or drug-using partners and family members. Alanon provides some immediate support and some useful insights.

Even though AA is the best we have at the moment, it is not good enough. Some studies show that about 22% of those seeking help from AA actually benefit (Fingarette, 1988). That means that we have failure in almost 80% of all cases. I dislike those odds. By the way, inpatient alcohol and drug programs demonstrate about the same success/failure rate—but more on that later.

The AA model rests on the assumption that alcoholism, for example, is a single disease, dictating a single approach to treatment. However, while the disease model of AA and other programs may be valid for some people, I do not buy it for all substance abusers. I and many others have seen too many clients who change without hitting bottom, who stop without detoxification, who are able to control their intake, etc. Furthermore, I believe that many substance abusers initially turn to alcohol or drugs as a solution to a problem and then find over time that that the solution has become the problem, quite apart from biological considerations.

Please don't go off and proclaim my notions as anti-AA, for they are not. I really believe that the AA philosophy helps many people and will continue to do so in the future. But people have become narrow, rigid, and evangelical about the AA approach, and this limits the exploration of additional treatment approaches.

Another area of misunderstanding and rigidity appears in

the area of "family treatment." Family therapists working with substance abusers seem to insist upon forcing people into roles that fit their theoretical models. Oftentimes families coming into treatment are "assigned" roles such as "enabler," "distractor," etc., and then forced to live up to these roles in family sessions. Bent on applying the latest in family treatment, the therapists and families miss the opportunity to get a handle on what might really abet change. I am afraid that some of the same mentality also exists with the current emphasis on adult children of alcoholics (ACOAs).

Despite the relative lack of success and high recidivism rate, why do programs, especially 30-day inpatient programs and intensive outpatient programs, continue to flourish? The answer is pure and simple: MONEY. The most expensive 30-day inpatient alcohol and drug programs can cost close to $30,000 per month. Some of the nonhospital residential programs cost half that. Yet, the Betty Ford clinic, which is nonprofit, does the job for about $6,000 per month. Sophisticated health care corporations, which own most psychiatric hospitals in major urban areas, have done a spectacular marketing job with corporate employee assistance departments and with insurance companies. They may not get high cure rates, but they have successfully established a system with high return and with a revolving population! With a zeal that rivals the disastrous implementation of traditional psychoanalytic models in community mental health centers in the 1960s and '70s, we have rushed in to do something, even when there is not clear evidence that it works! And we have made a lot of money for greedy corporations in the process.

Obviously these impediments to effective treatment apply to gay and straight clients alike. Gay and lesbian clients must jump additional hurdles. For one thing, gay-oriented treatment programs are few and far between. Gay men and women in AA groups as well as in inpatient settings often experience the same lack of acceptance that influenced their substance abuse in the first place. In cities like Atlanta, there are AA groups that are primarily gay, but the therapist must be aware that sometimes these groups become ingrown and lose their anonymity. Still, many gay and lesbian clients find the support they need from these AA experiences.

Another obstacle to effective treatment comes in the form of therapists who do not have the experience or the interest in working with homosexual clients. The rigid family approaches simply are not helpful with gay and lesbian couples. Perhaps some of the readers of this book will develop the expertise and flexibility to work effectively with gay alcoholism and drug abuse.

So what is my standard prescription for work with couples where there is a substance abuse problem? Again, since I do not feel that it is a single problem, I do not have a "standard approach." I will *not* work long-term with a couple where one partner or both are blatantly, actively alcoholic, for example. Where the alcohol or drug plays a critical role in dysfunctional system patterns, I *do* push for the available standard treatments. If I can at least get an alcoholic to agree that the substance use creates a problem that disrupts the relationship and to agree to do something about it, we may have some ingredients necessary for change.

If the partners refuse to accept alcohol as a major part of their relationship problem, I may have to tell them honestly that I am unable to help. In those circumstances, I may agree to a three- or four-session contract to explore their relationship and the effects of substance abuse. Sometimes they will return to treatment later and work more cooperatively.

Jeremy, 41, came to see me alone about a couple problem. His partner of 10 years was, he claimed, a nightly, heavy drinking alcoholic. Every evening after work they met at a bar, where David, 50, drank himself into oblivion. Jeremy was clearly tired of this pattern, and he also was concerned about David's health. His own drinking had been heavy, but he now held himself to one or two drinks per week. His own recent involvement in AA was also a strong motivation for seeking help. David, his partner, refused to come in to talk. He also stated clearly to Jeremy that he had no desire to stop drinking. Under those circumstances, I agreed to see Jeremy alone for a few sessions in order to explore more unilateral options.

Younger gay men sometimes find it difficult to give up a bar-oriented lifestyle with its glitter and energy. Chances are that they have met a lover in this setting and that that situation in common fuels the use of alcohol. Many of these young people have not gotten past the point of wanting immediate gratifications. The pounding beat of rock music, the energy of vital, cruising men, and the glitter of tight, young bodies dressed in the latest all serve to distract young people from the more difficult and seemingly mundane tasks of looking at one's life for meaning and planning for a future. Some are simply too young; the time has not come yet for focusing on more serious concerns. They may have burst out of their "straight" confines and want to savor this new life with every bit of energy at their command. Alcohol helps fuel their sexual awakening. Some men (fewer women) never grow out of this social scene. They hang onto the places where they once experienced fun and excitement, and they never can look beyond the bars to what life may hold for them. For them alcohol or drugs (and being gay) become a valuable tool for masking their shortcomings.

Some couples return over and over again to the bars where they met or where their friends still hang out. In small towns the bar may act as a kind of social center, a place to meet your friends and have a good time. In larger cities the function remains the same, but it may not be so intimate (it can be a way of hanging onto youth, which can become an obsession in this culture). In either case, alcohol and drugs can become the essence of a social life. Dealing with substance abuse becomes largely a matter of seeking alternatives to this social option. Developing new friends and new interests is crucial.

DOMESTIC VIOLENCE

A raging debate exists in certain professional circles over the most effective way of dealing with domestic violence. One school continues to promote more traditional views involving social control. This school may be opposed to treating a couple together and may promote group treatment for the "perpetrator." There is the threat that if the male perpetrator does not learn to control violent actions, he will go to jail.

The second school says that social control is not the answer, that domestic violence is a systemic problem based on issues of symmetry and complementarity in the relationship. This approach owes a lot to the thinking of the Milan group (Selvini Palazzoli, Boscolo, Cecchin, and Prata, 1978) refined and modified by Gerry Lane and Thomas Russell (1989). This school says essentially that no one is at fault, that the partners develop a "dance" that escalates to the point of explosion, which allows them to begin again from the start.

If you are involved in cases with domestic violence, I suggest that you review the relatively limited literature on this subject (Coleman and Straus, 1986; Straus and Gelles, 1986, 1989). As I mentioned earlier, I have little experience in working with couples where domestic violence is the central issue. I do, however, have some observations or speculations to make. One of the reasons that domestic violence receives so much attention is that it almost always involves a larger, stronger man attacking a smaller, weaker woman. We have a very strong prohibition in this country about men beating on women. Of course, realistically this violence leads to quite alarming and physically and emotionally destructive situations.

Gay and lesbian couples generally do not fit the larger/smaller configuration. Even if they did, it is doubtful that two men or two women fighting with each other would generate the level of concern aroused by a man beating on a woman. Gay and lesbian couples are concerned about violence between them, but it seems that the concern has little to do with "she's bigger and it's not a fair match." In addition, the authorities are less concerned about the goings-on between two homosexuals than they are about heterosexual domestic violence (although I did hear about a situation recently where a judge remanded two gay men to couples therapy as a result of the violence between them). Therefore, I will speculate that a lot of homosexual domestic violence goes unreported because it is not as great a concern for the people involved or for the authorities. It still befits you as a therapist to explore violence as an issue with same-sex couples, as an obvious disrupting influence in the relationship.

MENAGES À TROIS

I do not expect that as a therapist working with gay and lesbian couples you will be deluged by threesomes. I have seen exactly three such configurations in my years of working with same-sex couples. One involved three men, two of whom had been together for six years prior to adding number three. Number three got added because number one had turned increasingly to alcohol, and number three helped to fill the needs of an increasingly isolated number two. Ironically, they came into therapy when number one gave up his drinking to find that he was essentially a single man living with a couple.

The second situation involved two men in a 15-year relationship who added someone younger and more exotic. In the past, they had turned to agreed-upon outlets for outside sex and excitement. The AIDS crisis threatened that plan. They all came to see me for a "tune-up" to help prevent future problems in their new configuration.

The third scenario consisted of a bisexual man married to a woman, with whom he had been friends for years. She knew all about his gay involvements. They had settled upon an arrangement in their four-year-old marriage. He was free to see men on the side, and they both preferred that he be open about whom he was seeing or dating. She saw other men also, but proved more reluctant to share many of the details. Eventually, he began seeing another man on a regular basis and the three of them decided to live together. This arrangement was somewhat different from the other two in that the "head man" had sex with his wife and with his boyfriend, but the other two had no sexual contact with each other. (The situation had rather a harem quality to it, which increased certain dysfunction-causing pressures.)

When working with families where there are children, we have good working models for dealing with hierarchy and boundaries, even though they are usually out of kilter when the family comes to see us. In working with families where there are three adults sexually and emotionally involved, the issues of boundaries and hierarchy become more confusing. Obviously, with three adults sharing a household in this kind of situation the potential exists for rigid triangles. Who is in charge of what? Does each have equal status in the relationship? Who was there first? Does jealousy play a part? The therapist will stay busy sorting out boundaries in this kind of arrangement (and actually it is an engaging challenge to keep it all straight).

For the therapist, working with threesomes can prove confusing because you probably won't have much experience or literature to tell you what to do. It can also be fun because you have to use your own creativity in terms of helping them to design a workable model for themselves. Be careful that moral judgments or social expectations do not creep in and distort your potential for doing some good work.

CONCLUSIONS

You will undoubtedly come across situations, especially in working with substance abuse and domestic violence, where your skills get taxed to the limits or where you are really at a loss about where to go next. I wish I could help more with clear directives about the absolute best and foolproof ways of dealing in these areas. Unfortunately I cannot. I did say earlier that this exposition would not be a cookbook. It cannot be because I do not have the answers. Substance abuse, violence, unusual circumstances – all present challenges for the therapist that call for great creativity. My hope is that the material in this chapter, however brief, will help you dodge some of the pitfalls and encourage your creative instincts.

10

ENDINGS

As we come to the end of this book, I have some things to say about endings on several different levels. First, we must address the issue of the end of therapy and all of its implications. Second, we need to look at the ending of relationships or, at least, the ending of a relationship as it has formerly been defined. Third, we will discuss some conclusions we may draw from this book, as well as unanswered questions that may linger in working with same-sex couples.

ENDING THERAPY

Systems work in general should not generate the attachments that we see with one-to-one intrapsychic forms of therapy. This is not to say that attachments are not formed between therapist and clients, but if the job has been done well, terminating therapy need not be as traumatic or wrenching as sometimes happens in intrapsychic individual therapy. In addition, since you focus on a dyad in couples work, rather than the individual, and on interactions between the two of them, there is less dependence on the therapist. (Please understand that I am dealing in general, and not addressing issues such as a client's anger over some change that has been generated in therapy, the therapist's "clay feet," especially if the client has information or even fantasies about the therapist's relationships, etc., all of which need to be tackled in the general structure of the therapy process.)

Experienced therapists recognize that the beginnings and endings of therapy are fraught with vagaries. People miss initial, scheduled appointments and then call several months later, needing to be seen immediately. Clients may make many false starts – calling, canceling, coming alone for couples work, coming once and never returning, etc. Endings also are not always clear-cut; in fact, in many cases the lack of clear ending, up to a point, may pave the way for return visits at a time that feels more promising to the people involved. Since many clients feel that they cannot come back to therapy without carrying the onus of failure, I always end therapy with the assurance that it is okay to come back if the need arises. In fact, many couples will hit snags at developmental choice points that they have not even experienced at the time of the initial therapy. I tell them that hitting snags is no reflection on the work they have done so far. Good work in therapy may even enable them to sense snags before they develop into major problems.

The point is that a very structured beginning and ending may not be what you get to work with. My own feeling, not borne out by research, is that ambivalence about therapy may be more prevalent among gay and lesbian couples than among the population in general. Such attitudes as "gay relationships don't last anyway," and "you cannot trust the straight world," are deeply embedded in the subculture.

So sometimes the therapy ends by mutual consent, processed and agreed upon by client and therapist. (Usually I taper off the frequency of visits, going from once per week to every other week or once per month.) Sometimes the therapy ends by several "no shows." Sometimes the voice at the end of the telephone line informs you that they have decided not to continue for now, and no amount of convincing will get them in for a final session. Surprisingly, many of these ragged endings will result in a return to therapy when the couple feels ready. *Their* readiness is a more important factor than the evaluation of the therapist. (I tend to like the more relaxed approach to scheduling and ending that the Milan group has adopted.)

Of course, my comfort level is much higher when a couple and I agree to end therapy for the time being because we have reached some reasonably solid goals *at this point in time*. I do not discourage periodic check-ups. I encourage clients to use the skills we have worked on, as well as any mechanisms we may have developed, to avoid future pitfalls. If they get stuck, they are welcome to call.

ENDING RELATIONSHIPS

The connotations associated with ending a relationship are troublesome to me – troublesome because for most of us ending a relationship means generating a cutoff. It also has implications of anger, guilt, and unpleasantness. Sometimes negative factors follow a "breakup," but this need not be necessarily so.

I do not write this in the vein of a pollyanna. In working with divorcing or divorced parents, I have reached a certain level of success in enabling the relationship to continue between the parents in a different but important way: child management. Since marriage and parenting operate on several levels, it is possible to continue or to develop a very positive relationship in the arena of managing and raising children *without* having a spousal connection. Not only does this develop a more positive environment for the children, but it also helps the parents experience some sense of accomplishment from the years that they have spent together. Often they can avoid many of the feelings of failure and even *like* each other in the process. Some couples are able to work out cooperative management while recognizing that as lovers and friends they just cannot succeed. (It also follows that some couples do great as spouses while having problems as co-managers.)

The child issue is not so prominent with same-sex couples, but many of them develop strong "family" ties with their partners. When the relationship seems no longer to fill their needs on some level, they are all too ready to give up *all* aspects of their lives together – to cut off from their former partners as family. Sometimes the feeling of betrayal and animosity surrounding a transition do not permit working on other aspects of the relationship. But there are more opportunities than one might expect, especially given the limited supports available to many gay men and lesbians. In addition, it may be helpful to convey to your same-sex couples that, not only do they *not* need to buy into marriage models from the straight world, but also they need to avoid a divorce mentality that stems from the same models. As we discussed earlier, marriage models have all kinds of pitfalls that same-sex couples can avoid.

Two men I have worked with have recently decided to split after 14 years together. This is not a hasty decision. They first began to grapple with it two years ago. When they first met they were 18 and 24. Their needs have diverged over the years, but they have still grown up together. That should be worth quite a bit. The therapy challenge becomes one of discovering what kind of new relationship they can forge with each other.

As silly as it sounds, one of the problems with transitions like this involves semantics. We do not have really good terminology to suggest that a relationship continues in a different form. For the couple above, they have experienced a lot of pressure in the community because of their visibility as role models. Others see the change as the failure of yet another same-sex couple. The fact that they hope to forge a supportive arrangement for themselves sounds like a rationalization.

As my colleague Michael Milligan puts it, our culture is hooked on "one true way to be together." Anything else implies disloyalty and failure. These perceptions impose limitations on all couples, same-sex and heterosexual.

One very effective technique for dealing with transitions involves the creation of a ritual that will mark the passage. Jay Haley (1984) has pioneered the technique, among others (Imber-Black, Roberts, and Whiting, 1988; Madanes, 1981). Rituals work for joining and separating as well as for marking significant change in a relationship. Couples who have never accepted the lifestyle change that accompanied the birth of their children get stuck at some point along the line. He feels neglected; she feels unsupported in her role as a mother. Once the couple can accept that things really have changed, a ritual can help them move on with their lives together. Couples are not ready for rituals until they really can accept that things have changed.

Same-sex couples have very few rituals for consolidating their relationships or for marking transitions, so their creation becomes even more important. One couple, who decided to live and love apart after 10 years, found value in the following ritual. They had taken masses of photographs over the 10 years, but had never organized them. The ending ritual involved going away to a favorite place for the weekend with their photographs and two albums. They spent the weekend reminiscing, laughing, crying, and making this transition. At the end of the weekend, each went her separate way with an album of her own.

Please heed that rituals should be very specific to a couple's experience, so it is important that the partners have a significant part in designing them.

We all see our share of nasty, hostile situations that therapy cannot help resolve. Too often, especially with men, the transition is handled by getting involved with someone else. This is a ritual of sorts, but not a very productive one for either person in the relationship. Try to convince the newly enamored member of that! For him everything is beautiful, and he will not want to put his heart into a parting ritual. At some later time, when he presumably will have regrets about the abruptness of change, his former partner may be in no mood to get re-involved for the sake of ritual. My only suggestion is to predict this outcome in situations that warrant it.

If you excuse the prosaic metaphor, life is like a book, and a significant relationship takes up a chapter in it. Rather than tear the chapter up and discard it, our goal is to bring it to a smooth conclusion and to include its lessons as a useful backdrop for later chapters. (Remember, too, if your entire life is composed of a single chapter, it is a narrow life indeed.)

AIDS often leads to a different kind of termination – the death of a lover. While the couple may prepare for this in therapy, the grieving does not really become acute until after the death. While there is a certain amount of pain that is only dispelled with time, there are some things to attend to around an AIDS-related death.

Ritual can play an important part in the grieving process. In Chapter 8 we discussed the abruptness with which families often deal with the death of a son from AIDS. Bodies are whisked away to home towns, where friends and relatives knew nothing about the lifestyle of the deceased. Families hide cause of death. They conduct as little ritual as possible and invent more acceptable illnesses as the cause of death. Friends of the couple, back in the city of residence, are often cutoff from any mourning ritual.

Several years ago a close friend died while I was out of town. He had been hospitalized for several weeks, but few people knew how desperate his situation was (he carried an ARC diagnosis). When I returned the day after his death, his body had been flown back to his home city. No one ever received any information about a funeral from the family. I felt compelled to organize a memorial service, so that those of us who had been close to him could have some sort of ritual to mark his passage from this earth. We could not include his family because of the cutoff they had helped to generate.

The transition is eased a bit when the network has been established before death. It opens up some communication between family and friends. It provides a lot of support. It can serve to make things easier for the remaining partner. More than anything else I can think of, an established "formal" network offers the best available resource for everyone involved.

The remaining spouse – especially without the help of the

prearranged networking process – will most likely experience a great deal of loneliness. (Sometimes this is accompanied by a sense of relief, if the illness has been long and lingering.) Now the living partner must cope with a limited support network in general, and eventually with a limited pool of available singles, when it comes time to explore another relationship. In larger cities, support groups exist that can be quite helpful in the process, especially because others who are going through the same grieving process can readily identify with the special conditions that surround an AIDS death. Despite efforts at education, there remains a good deal of stigma associated with having coupled with someone who has died from AIDS.

ENDING THIS BOOK

We all have a lot to learn about working with couples. Our working with same-sex couples has been hampered by ignorance fostered by a number of factors, including lack of visibility of same-sex couples, lack of interest on the part of therapists, who focus on other populations, and lack of trust among gay men and lesbians, who still look at the straight world with a jaundiced eye. This book was written so that therapists would not begin doing therapy with same-sex couples with the erroneous assumption that information about couples in general would suffice. I mentioned at the beginning of the book that you do not have to be a gay or lesbian therapist to work successfully with gay and lesbian clients. Sometimes these clients would prefer a therapist with the same or similar sexual orientation, but a demonstration of your competence and understanding generally will suffice. (Some gay men prefer women therapists and often work with lesbians; the opposite is seldom true for lesbian clients.)

Apart from lack of information, outright prejudice still derails efforts to make good therapy available to same-sex couples. Lest you think I exaggerate, I present a letter which appeared in the December 1989 issue of the American Association for Marriage and Family Therapy's newspaper, *Family Therapy News*:

> I found the article on "Gay/Lesbian Workshops, Events to be Highlighted at Conference" (*Family Therapy News*, July/August) to be appalling to me, both personally and professionally. It appears that gays/lesbians/bisexuals are being perceived of as being healthy or normal, since this is being "highlighted" (and even allowed) at the AAMFT national conference. To many of us clinicians, gays/lesbians/bisexuals are not psychologically healthy, certainly not normal, and should not be permitted to be part of any conference put on by a national organization whose main purpose is to promote healthy families. How can this promote healthy families?
>
> As an associate member of the AAMFT, I would like to attend an AAMFT national conference. However, I will not attend one because I will not support any part of gay/lesbian/bisexual activities. Nor will I attend any future conference or events which allow gay/lesbian/bisexual activities.
>
> (Male person), M.A.

It is a fact that there are many people out there who think like this man. They are therapists and will work at some time with a "gay/lesbian/bisexual" person, because, even though they say that they have no interest in working with anything smacking of homosexuality, clients will come to them who need to deal with these issues. The narrowness of such therapists impedes any reasonable therapy process. Unfortunately, I am sure that the therapist who wrote this letter, after looking at the title of my book, would be loathe to even pick it up. The process of dispelling ignorance through education may go fairly quickly; the process of dispelling prejudice goes so slowly.

Frankly I am pleased at having written this book. I am also humbled at realizing how much more I have to learn, and somewhat chastened at not being able to provide good recommendations for some of the problems I have identified. But it is a start. Still, very pressing questions remain unanswered. What do you do in areas that lack social resources? What will happen to the direction of gay rights? How do you tackle built-in prejudices on the part of the public and client alike? Will there be a cure for AIDS?

I also have stated several times that this would not be a cookbook, and I have refrained from presenting what I consider to be tedious case examples that dwell on every nuance of a session. Your good sense and experience will help fill in the gaps in your own style; perhaps you will come up with a more creative solution to a situation than I ever would have!

Finally, I admit to a "hidden agenda." I would truly like to see more systems thinking in this area and in all aspects of psychotherapy. Most people working with gays and lesbians have concentrated more on intrapsychic aspects, which, while they may be useful, often are not helpful and efficient in helping people move toward solutions to their problems. I know that this is heresy to some, but intelligent people with good information may do a better job of solving problems than those professionals bent on protecting their areas of turf. Endless discussions of the nuance of diagnosis, the efficacy of certain tests, and the speculative combinations of medication do not benefit people looking for help with change. A systems approach sidesteps a lot of professional nonsense and leads more quickly to change.

I hope after reading this book you experience a new sense of competence when working with the gay and lesbian couples who need you help!

REFERENCES

CHAPTER 1. DEFINING POPULATIONS
AND PRACTICES

Kinsey, A. C. (1941). Homosexuality: Criteria for a hormonal explanation of the homosexual. *Journal of Clinical Endocrinology, 1*, 424–428.

Kinsey, A. C., Pomeroy, W. B., & Martin, C. E. (1948). *Sexual behavior in the human male*. Philadelphia: W. B. Saunders Company.

Tripp, C. A. (1975). *The homosexual matrix*. New York: McGraw-Hill.

CHAPTER 2. THE ETIOLOGY OF HOMOSEXUALITY

Adams, H. E., & Sturgis, E. T. (1977). Status of behavioral reorientation techniques in the modification of homosexuality: A review. *Psychological Bulletin, 84*(6), 1171–1188.

Bell, A. P., Weinberg, M. S., & Hammersmith, S. K. (1981). *Sexual preference: Its development in men and women*. Bloomington: Indiana University Press.

Bieber, I., Dain, H. J., Dince, P. R., Drellich, M. G., Grand, H. G., Gundlach, R. H., Kremer, M. W., Rifkin, A. H., Wilbur, C. B., & Bieber, T. B. (1962). *Homosexuality: A psychoanalytic study*. New York: Basic Books.

Coates, S., & Person, E. S. (1985). Extreme boyhood femininity: Isolated behavior or pervasive disorder? *Journal of the American Academy of Child Psychiatry, 24*(6), 702–709.

Dorner, G., Rohde, W., Stahl, F., Krell, L., & Masius, W. G. (1975). A neuroendocrine predisposition for homosexuality in men. *Archives of Sexual Behavior, 4*(1), 1–8.

Ellis, L., & Ames, M. A. (1987). Neurohormonal functioning and sexual orientation: A theory of homosexuality-heterosexuality. *Psychological Bulletin, 101*(2), 233–258.

Ellis, L., Ames, M. A., Peckham, W., & Burke, D. (1988). Sexual orientation of human offspring may be altered by severe maternal stress during pregnancy. *Journal of Sex Research, 25*(1), 152–157.

Evans, R. B. (1971). Parental relationships and homosexuality. *Medical Aspects of Human Sexuality, 5,* 164–177.

Feinberg, J. (1987). *Sexual orientation and three-generational family patterns.* Unpublished doctoral dissertation, Georgia State University, Atlanta.

Freud, S. (1921). Group psychology and the analysis of the ego. In J. Strachey (Ed. and Trans.), *The standard edition of the complete psychological works of Sigmund Freud* (Vol. 18, pp. 67–144). New York: W. W. Norton.

Freud, S. (1905). Three essays on the theory of sexuality. In J. Strachey (Ed. and Trans.), *The standard edition of the complete psychological works of Sigmund Freud* (Vol. 7, pp. 123–243). New York: W. W. Norton.

Friedman, R. C. (1988). *Male homosexuality: A contemporary psychoanalytic perspective.* New Haven: Yale University Press.

Green, R. (1976). One-hundred ten feminine and masculine boys: Behavioral contrasts and demographic similarities. *Archives of Sexual Behavior, 5*(5), 425–446.

Green, R. (1979). Childhood cross-gender behavior and subsequent sexual preference. *American Journal of Psychiatry, 136*(1), 106–108.

Green, R. (1985). Gender identity in childhood and later sexual orientation: Follow-up of 78 males. *American Journal of Psychiatry, 142*(3), 339–341.

Jones, E. (1955). *The life and work of Sigmund Freud, Vol. 2.* New York: Basic. 278–281.

Kallman, F. J. (1952). Comparative twin study on the genetic aspects of male homosexuality. *Journal of Nervous and Mental Disease, 115*(4), 283–298.

Kolodny, R., Masters, W., Hendryx, J., & Toro, G. (1971). Plasma testosterone and semen analysis in male homosexuals. *New England Journal of Medicine, 285,* 1170–1174.

MacCulloch, M. J., & Waddington, J. L. (1981). Neuroendocrine mechanisms and the aetiology of male and female homosexuality. *British Journal of Psychiatry, 139,* 341–345.

Mesnikoff, A. M., Rainer, J. D., Kolb, L. C., & Carr, A. C. (1963). Intrafamilial determinants of divergent sexual behavior in twins. *American Journal of Psychiatry, 119,* 732–738.

Rainer, J. D., Mesnikoff, A., Kolb, L. C., & Carr, A. (1960). Homosexuality and heterosexuality in identical twins. *Psychosomatic Medicine, 22*(4), 251–260.

West, D. J. (1959). Parental figures in the genesis of male homosexuality. *International Journal of Social Psychiatry, 5,* 85–97.

Zuger, B. (1974). Effeminate behavior in boys: Parental age and other factors. *Archives of General Psychiatry, 30,* 173–177.

CHAPTER 3. PRECOUPLING CONSIDERATIONS

Blumstein, P. & Schwartz, P. (1983). *The American couple*. New York: Morrow.

Bowen, M. (1976). Theory in the practice of psychotherapy. In P. Guerin (Ed.), *Family therapy theory and practice*. New York: Gardner Press.

Fricke, A. (1981). *Reflections of a rock lobster*. New York: Alyson.

Kerr, M. E. & Bowen, M. (1988). *Family evaluation*. New York: W. W. Norton.

Mendola, M. (1980). *The Mendola Report*. New York: Crown.

CHAPTER 4. COUPLING ISSUES

Berger, M., Foster, M., & Wallston, B. S. (1978). Finding two jobs. In R. Rapaport & R. Rapaport (Eds.), *Working couples*. New York: Harper & Row.

Berger, M., Foster, M., & Wallston, B. S. (1977). You and me against the world: Dual career couples and joint job seeking. *Journal of Research and Development in Education, 4*, 30–36.

Blumstein, P. & Schwartz, P. (1983). *The American couple*. New York: Morrow.

Krestan, J. & Bepko, C. S. (1980). The problem of fusion in lesbian relationships. *Family Process, 19*(3), 277–289.

Haley, J. (1987). *Problem-solving therapy*, 2nd ed. San Francisco: Jossey-Bass.

Haley, J. (1973). *Uncommon therapy*. New York: W. W. Norton.

McGoldrick, M. & Gerson, R. (1985). *Genograms in family assessment*. New York: W. W. Norton.

CHAPTER 5. SOME THEORETICAL AND PRACTICAL ISSUES IN COUPLES COUNSELING

Bandler, R. & Grinder, J. (1975). *The structure of magic*. Palo Alto: Science and Behavior Books.

Minuchin, S. (1974). *Families and family therapy*. Cambridge, MA: Harvard University Press.

Watzlawick, P., Weakland, J., & Fisch, R. (1974). *Change*. New York: W. W. Norton.

CHAPTER 6. SOME INTERVENTIONS

Bowen, M. (1978). *Family therapy in clinical practice*. New York: Aronson.

McWhirter, D. P. & Mattison, A. M. (1984). *The male couple.* Englewood Cliffs, NJ: Prentice-Hall.
Silverstein, C. (1981). *Man to man.* New York: Morrow.
Zilbergeld, B. (1978). *Male sexuality.* Boston: Little, Brown.

CHAPTER 8. THE ISSUE OF AIDS

Kübler-Ross, E. (1969). *On death and dying.* New York: Macmillan.
Landau-Stanton, J. (1983). Link Therapy. Workshop at the International Family Therapy Conference, Brussels.
Stanton, M. D. & Todd, T. (1982). *The family therapy of drug abuse and addiction.* New York: Guilford Press.

CHAPTER 9. ALCOHOL, DRUGS, AND ADDITIONAL THERAPY CONCERNS

Coleman, D. & Straus, M. (1986). Marital power, conflict and violence in a nationally represented sample of American couples. *Violence and Victims, 1*(2).
Fingarette, H. (1988). *Heavy drinking: The myth of alcoholism as a disease.* Berkeley: University of California Press.
Lane, G. & Russell, T. (1989). Second-order systems work with violent couples. In P. Caesar & K. Hamberger (Eds.), *Treating men who batter.* New York: Springer.
Selvini Palazzoli, M., Boscolo, L., Cecchin, G., & Prata, G. (1978). *Paradox and counterparadox.* New York: Aronson.
Straus, M. & Gelles, R. (August, 1986). Societal change and family violence 1975–1985 as provided by two national surveys. *Journal of Marital and Family Therapy, 48,* 465–469.
Straus, M. & Gelles, R. (1989). *Physical violence in the American family.* New Brunswick: Transaction Books.

CHAPTER 10. ENDINGS

Imber-Black, E., Roberts, J., & Whiting, D. (1988). *Rituals in families and family therapy.* New York: W. W. Norton.
Haley, J. (1984). *Ordeal therapy.* San Francisco: Jossey-Bass.
Letter to the editor (December 1989). *Family Therapy News.*
Madanes, C. (1981). *Strategic family therapy.* San Francisco: Jossey-Bass.

INDEX

159